Experiments on Reality

Tim Robinson

PENGUIN

IRELAND

PENGUIN IRELAND

UK | USA | Canada | Ireland | Australia
India | New Zealand | South Africa

Penguin Ireland is part of the Penguin Random House group of companies
whose addresses can be found at global.penguinrandomhouse.com.

First published 2019
001

Copyright © Tim Robinson, 2019

The moral right of the author has been asserted

Set in 13.5/17.75pt Perpetua Std
Typeset by Jouve (UK), Milton Keynes
Printed and bound in Great Britain by Clays Ltd, Elcograf S.p.A.

A CIP catalogue record for this book is available from the British Library

ISBN: 978-1-844-88483-4

www.greenpenguin.co.uk

MIX
Paper from
responsible sources
FSC® C018179
www.fsc.org

Penguin Random House is committed to a
sustainable future for our business, our readers
and our planet. This book is made from Forest
Stewardship Council® certified paper.

Contents

Preface

Most of these texts have an initiating mechanism, a strange device, a detonator, to blow them away into neighbouring geographies of memory, autobiographical fantasy, or, in one case at least, a desert of daftness. (Some notes on this matter are at the back of the book.) My focus is, as always, on the multitudinous ways in which our physical bodies relate to the physical universe. This commitment to material nature in its wondrous plenitude encourages me to reappropriate terms, themes and tones long regarded as the property of religion, and dares me to denounce supernaturalism as blasphemy.

The rest of the book is taken up by two longer pieces. 'Backwards and Digressive' is an account of the evolution of the visual art of my other self, Tim Drever. 'A Land Without Shortcuts' is an overtly environmentalist lecture, functioning here as a concluding (if not conclusive) rattle of drums.

From my horrified and fascinated teenage reading of Sartre's *La Nausée* I remember Roquentin, the novel's protagonist, picking up a stone and revealing a bare patch of sticky mud, which to him represented the disgusting truth of the matter, of matter itself, utterly alien to human existence. I wanted gently to disengage that stone from his grip and carefully replace it in its grassy nest, so healing the rift between humankind and the inanimate. But the belief behind that urge was not animism. The distinction between the animate and the inanimate has been hard-won and is foundational. Some believe that mountains are conscious; I cannot imagine why one would even want to believe such an absurdity. While few thinkers would claim to have answered 'the hard question' of consciousness, science is beginning to find its way about the soft labyrinth of the brain, the material foundation of mentality. Disembodied life after death is another belief I find aesthetically unattractive. The course of evolution that brought us forth from cosmic dust is a sequence of marvels the contemplation of which has dazzled and delighted me all my life, and it is demeaned by the spiritualist claim that the soul can exist without the support of matter, as it were by divine conjuring. No, there is only one world, and that is all we need to know.

Tim Robinson, August 2018

Hunter-gatherers

When I was about eleven and my brother eight, our parents took themselves off for a short caravan holiday, leaving us in charge of the house, the hens, and ourselves. Looking back, I suspect my father was going through one of the bouts of depression he reckoned struck him down every five years, and that the caravanning was undertaken in obedience to our family doctor's orders, in those days when doctors were trusted friends who ordered one to do what one wanted to do in any case. But at the time we had no understanding of his condition, and we waved the pair of them off with glee. The weather was fine, the countryside (watery intricacies of Wharfedale and airy uplands of Ilkley Moor in Yorkshire) intimately known to us. As to feeding ourselves, the War had been over for a year or two, rationing restrictions were being relaxed, and we planned to indulge our newfound taste for bacon and eggs followed by 'Same again!'

As soon as the parents were gone we jumped on our bikes and pedalled a few miles between green hayfields and little woods to Addingham Scar, a steep limestone crag, tree-grown, that scrambles down from the lane above to the banks of the River Wharfe. This was a favourite and almost secret adventure-world for us; passers-by on the lane might remain unaware of the great rocky slope falling away from them unless they peered through the roadside hedge, and from the opposite bank of the river it was shrouded in birch trees. Once we caught a large (record-breaking, we reckoned) slow-worm over a foot long here, a smooth flexuous bar of silver; we kept it for some time, feeding it on slugs, and it used to rest coiled around my wrist like a sleep-heavy bracelet. On another occasion we turned over a stone and disturbed a cluster of young slow-worms just a couple of inches long and of the tint and texture of bronze. We brought a few of these away with us, but they soon escaped through chinks in their new cardboard home. (Fifteen or so years later, in the Grand Bazaar of Istanbul, I was to buy my beloved a snake bracelet of coiled metal wire the colour of old gold, said to have come out of revolutionary Russia hidden in the clothing of a rich émigré, because it reminded me of those lovely longlost creatures. It too was flexuous, and in addition it had eyes of tiny rubies, and a row of small blue beads down its spine. But not everyone loves such things: 'Imagine having a snake on your wrist!' she shuddered. So it rests with me, one of hardly a dozen life-deep treasures.)

On this occasion we had no luck on the Scar and

decided to explore a little stream hidden among trees on the other side of the lane above. There were two or three houses nearby and we were not quite sure we were on public land, so we moved cautiously. The stream was shrunken from a long period of dry weather. Its landlocked pools and flowery banks were abuzz with insect life. Damselflies hung in the air like tiny blue neon signs, water boatmen sculled purposefully to and fro on still water faces, water beetle larvae lurked submerged among slimy weeds. All these little creatures, and dozens more, were familiar to me; I still have *An Insect Book for the Pocket* (OUP, 1946), in which I looked them up as I came across them and on the fly-leaves of which I listed those I had seen, under their Latin names, in a juvenile block-letter script. My long-suffering mother used to complain that the scorpion-like dragonfly larvae living in a jamjar on a window ledge by the kitchen door frightened the milkman by goggling at him with bulgy eyes. I pressed my brother and his little friends into service to scour heathery acres of Ilkley Moor in search of silky brown-haired caterpillars of the northern eggar moth and the fat green caterpillars with pink warts of the emperor moth. Even minute translucent gnat larvae, hanging head-down by a breathing tube in their tails from the surface-film of a cupful of water in a neglected flowerpot, did not escape my fascinated gaze. These little beings and the secretive nooks they inhabited remain vivid in my mind, to the point of

5

hyper-reality; writing about them now, nearly a lifetime later, both fixes and falsifies them, like pinned butterfly corpses in a cabinet.

But that day by the stream above the Scar brought us bigger game. A sudden turbulence in a pond cut off by falling water levels alerted us to the presence of a fish. We peered, and made it out, lying on the bottom, sleek brown against glistening pebbles: a sizeable trout. We considered the problem. Would it be legal to take it? Were we trespassing, in fact? And then we had nothing to catch it with or put it in if we succeeded; the idea of attacking it with sticks unnerved us. But what a prize to greet our parents with on their return, if we could make it ours! We cycled home thoughtfully, and made our plans.

We were up early the following morning. We located our father's landing net – he was a very occasional angler – and unscrewed its long handle. With the net itself disguised in a towel and strapped to the crossbar of my brother's bike, and the handle to mine, we slid silently into the silent dawn. Keeping low, out of sight of the nearby houses, we crept down through the little wood to the stream. The fish was still there. Voices of men coming along the lane above made us flatten ourselves to the stream bank for a panicky while until they passed. Then we screwed its handle onto the landing net, and in no time at all the trout was ours. We must have banged its head with a stone – I do not remember that – and soon we were tearing homewards, triumphant.

The first thing to be done was to measure it with the tape that lived in a drawer of my mother's sewing machine. Could we honestly say without exaggeration that it was over a foot long? We reckoned so. Then, did we gut it? Or did we shy away from the horrid business? I don't remember. A few days were due to elapse before our parents came home; every day we sniffed the fish anxiously. When at last they arrived, we capered round them as they inspected the catch and marvelled at our skill and bravery. That evening the great trout was consumed – either our fish, or a fresh one discreetly sourced from the local fishmonger's to replace it, unknown to us.

On Ilkley Moor

It was Ilkley, a small, prim town in the Yorkshire Dales, the heir to a fashionable spa of Victorian times, that incubated my interminable adolescence. Delirious hordes of ecstatic corpuscles raged through my veins in those days. One moonlit night in high summer they goaded me into slipping out of the house, almost running up Parish Ghyll, the steep residential road we lived on, and through the three little wooded parks that cling to the skirts of Ilkley Moor. Ahead, the sky had to muster all its stars to differentiate itself from the hulking mass of the moorland plateau. I pressed onwards up shaggy heather steeps and across dells breast-high in bracken, to the line of low cliffs and scarps that announces the wide wild acres beyond them. Out of breath, I paused to look back at the dim glimmers and roving sparks of the somnolent town below. A misshapen moon, almost full, hung above it. I found that in my violent scramble I had cut my finger on the razor-blade spine of a bracken stem, and blood was oozing, slowly. I raised my arm until my finger was silhouetted against the moon's disc, and watched as a black beadlet swelled and then fell as if cut off by its sharp edge. Appeased by the blood-sacrifice, I wrapped a handkerchief round my finger and began to pick my way home.

Ilkley Moor has been made world-famous by a dismal Yorkshire dialect song, 'On Ilkla Mooar baht 'at', that used to make me ashamed when, in the course of school trips to the Continent, we Ilkley Grammar School pupils met up with foreign school groups who could enchant us with lovely songs from the Auvergne, the Black Forest or Connemara, while we could find nothing better than this tedious rigmarole. However, the story that unfolds in the first lines of its verses, each followed by a triple dose of 'On Ilkla Mooar baht 'at', has a certain down-to-earth truth in it:

> Tha's been a cooartin' Mary Jane
> > On Ilkla Mooar baht 'at
> > On Ilkla Mooar baht 'at
> > On Ilkla Mooar baht 'at
> Tha's bahn' to catch thy deeath o' cowd
>
> Then us'll ha' to bury thee
> Then t'worms'll come an' eyt thee up
> Then t'ducks'll come an' eyt up t'worms
> Then us'll go an' eyt up t'ducks
>
> Then us'll all ha' etten thee
>
> That's wheear we get us ooan back.

In my schooldays a teaspoonful still survived of the folk-world of this song, in a few lanes of small houses that geographically and socially lay on the other side of the railway embankment from the three-floors-over-basement gentility of Parish Ghyll, and have long been swept away. There I found cramped but friendly kitchens and interesting backyards with ferret-hutches and tethered dogs. My friend Jim lived here; my mother disapproved of him, and another mark of his superior status was the jackdaw that rode on his shoulder and accompanied our caterpillar-hunts on the Moor. On one of these expeditions we found a fledgling, probably from a curlew's or a golden plover's nest, that had been mauled by a predator. After some debate we decided that it had to be killed. Jim picked it up and deftly twisted its head off as casually as if he were opening a screw-top bottle. Then he held the head up before him, beak to nose, and apologized to the little creature in a few serious and fitting words, which, regrettably, I do not remember, but which were as unsentimental about the cycles of birth and death as the folk song.

The old song lent itself to parody, at least. When a noticeably well-formed girl named Mattingham or something like it joined my class in the middle of a term, the less mannerly of us were soon singing 'On Ilkla Mooar with Matt'. While I was probably the only member of the class who spent much time on the Moor, I was too inhibited for it to be an arena for even the most juvenile groping towards the satisfaction of lust. Once with a girl who was vaguely identified as my girlfriend of that period I climbed the Moor to an abandoned quarry. A fine drizzle filled the rocky void plus the time spent in it with damp. At a loss, I stood disconsolately throwing pebbles into a puddle. The girl observed me curiously, and then pronounced, as if she were giving the scene its title: 'Tim, disconsolately throwing pebbles into a puddle.' Later we began a tentative game of tag; I chased her round the puddles; we slipped in mud and laughed and shrieked – but I took care never to catch her inescapably.

It was not until the early years of my life-partnership with M that the Moor revealed – but chastely – an erotic potential. We were in Ilkley to visit my parents in the family home, and had escaped from the tensions of the domestic situation by climbing to the crest of the Moor, just above the cliff and the huge cube of rock fallen from it known as the Cow and Calf. There we had a row, but made it up sufficiently well to continue our walk. It was a very hot day in a dry season, and in one place up on the plateau we noticed threads of smoke rising from the turf underfoot. We were a long way from any source of help, so we set about stamping out the incipient blaze, which seemed to transfer itself underground to another spot nearby. Eventually we managed to stand on all necks of the monster simultaneously, and went on our way uneasily aware that the first puff of wind could resurrect the fire.

A mile or so further on we paused to admire the feather-light, snow-white heads of countless bog-cotton plants filling a damp hollow. They flickered and wavered like cool flames. On impulse I took off all my clothes and waded out to sit among their soft caresses. M did not join me, but her alert gaze was enough to mend the distance left between us by our smouldering disagreement. Soon, though, it felt as if all the long bare horizons of the Moor were watching us, and I came out of the pale shape-shifting otherworld to join her on firmer ground.

How I Learned to
Love the Police

In the late sixties M and I were living in West Hampstead, London. Most of our friends were left-leaning artists, but one evening we found ourselves at a party of a more radical tone. I chatted to a young woman who told me she worked with the Black Panthers. I said I'd thought that the Black Panthers would not accept help from a white person. 'That's *their* problem!' she replied. I was impressed by this, and on parting I told her that if ever I could be of use, to give me a ring – and then, no doubt, I forgot about the matter.

A few days later came a telephone call. It seemed that on the previous evening the police had raided the Mangrove, a Caribbean restaurant run by a civil rights activist in Notting Hill, and a number of black customers had been arrested and charged with possession of cannabis. Would I please come to Marylebone courthouse tomorrow morning and help bail them out? I had no idea of what this entailed, but I promised to be there. It was raining heavily as I hurriedly dressed to leave the house next day, and at the last moment I threw on the most waterproof item to catch my eye: a second-hand policeman's cape.

The foyer of the courthouse was packed with an excited throng, nearly all black. Tough-looking young men were gleefully showing each other newspaper photographs in which they figured. At intervals around the walls policemen were leaning, heads down, avoiding eye contact, but showing off their biceps. Two tall, bowed figures stood in a corner as if they were pretending to be pot-plants, keeping their backs to the press photographers; I recognized Vanessa and Corin Redgrave. After some time, those offering to stand bail were called for. I found myself in a long queue moving steadily forward through two glass double doors and up the central aisle of the courtroom, as bail terms were agreed for one after another of the accused. I had some banknotes in my pocket, but I couldn't see what was going on ahead and had no idea of what would be expected of me when my turn should come. Fortunately someone ahead of me in the queue forestalled me by standing bail for all the remaining accused. I felt momentarily disappointed; I believe I had indulged a brief fantasy of being conducted down into the dungeons of the courthouse, shown the caged prisoners, and saying, 'I'll take that one.' Instead, we superfluous ones turned about and began to file out of the court. Policemen politely held open the two glass double doors for us.

But no sooner was I past the first pair of doors than

they were slammed behind me and the second pair slammed ahead of me, and I found myself in a glass cell, as it were, with a belligerent policeman. He pointed at the damp bundle under my arm: my policeman's cape. Where did I get it? In Portobello market, I replied. He studied me closely, asked what I did. 'I'm a freelance technical illustrator,' I said. He suddenly bellowed, 'Does that mean you *work*?' I stood on my dignity: Yes, I did work, and there was no need to shout. 'Well, I'm just trying to make you out,' he grumbled. He looked frustrated; it was clear that he had no more idea than I had as to the legality of my possession of a second-hand policeman's cape. He soon gave up, and rapped on the door ahead of me. It was flung open, and I was spat out, into freedom.

As the Cicada Sings It

One sunny day I strode out from Carcassonne along the towpath of Louis XIV's great Canal du Midi. After a while the roar of the main road that followed the canal for a mile or so took itself off, and another noise made itself felt. A crackling as if the world was being electrocuted like a bluebottle in a flytrap – but prolonged remorselessly. A seething as if the sunlight itself was sizzling, like drops of water on hot stones – but with a beat to it, an insistent rhythm, a purposive scansion. It came from all directions and none, and at first, in this lonely spot, was almost frightening. I remembered what I had read, many years ago, in one of J.-H. Fabre's books on entomology. This was the famous massed choir of the *cigale,* the cicada, turning the sun's rays into sound.

The individual cicada has astonishing noisemaking capacities. On either side of its abdomen the exoskeleton, its husk, is modified into membranous organs that produce a rapid series of clicks; the abdomen itself is largely hollow and acts as a resonance chamber. The result is a dry rattle that fades and dies in a minute or so and is soon repeated. And where there are hordes of these insects, the aggregated noise is continuous and intense.

That walk in Languedoc, where, as in Fabre's Provence, every tree and bush is full of these little beasts, was my first exposure to the paired phenomena of midday sun and the sun-fuelled insects' clamour. The vast flat pulsating countryside seemed to focus itself on me as if I were the only audience for its raging. I passed the wide entrance to a yard surrounded by the outhouses of an old grange that looked as if it were deserted. I lingered. The waves of sound wrapped around the place like an enchantment; no dog ran out to greet or threaten me; no mysterious girl was glimpsed in this lost domain. The cicadas continued their inane racket. Soon I turned back towards the gothic turrets of the town.

Jean-Henri Fabre meant a great deal to me in my childhood, although I was an amateur of 'bugs and slugs', as unkind friends put it, long before I read *Fabre's Book of Insects*, which like all his popular works is based on his monumental *Souvenirs Entomologiques* (1879–1909). Only recently, from an exhibition in the Jardin des Plantes in Paris, have I acquired an image of him, an elderly though upright man wearing a broad-brimmed soft hat that suggests the country *curé*, with surprised eyebrows, precise lips and an inquisitive nose. When as a youngster I lay down to watch the comings and goings of some fluffy little solitary bees that had made their burrows in a patch of clay by the path, on Ilkley Moor, I already knew from Fabre that they would stock them with caterpillars on which they would lay their eggs, and that their larvae would eat the caterpillars, which had not been killed but paralysed by bee-stings. And when another sort of bee arrived, a slim, black-and-yellow banded one that looked like a miniature wasp, I knew it was a parasite looking for a chance to enter one of the burrows and lay its own eggs in it. (I captured one of these cuckoo insects and kept it for a few days in a jamjar, and made what I hoped was an original discovery, that it slept sticking out at right-angles to a twig which it held onto not with its legs but its mandibles. Of course this behaviour must have been well known to Fabre and earlier naturalists.)

Two chapters stand out for me in my memories of Fabre's writings: 'The Pine Processionary' and 'The Night of the Great Peacock'. Pine Processionary caterpillars follow each other nose to tail when moving from a pine branch they have eaten bare to a fresh one, or from tree to tree; the leader (which finds itself in this role just by chance) gropes around and eventually moves forward, laying down a silken thread from the spinnerets on its face as a guide to its followers, each of which adds its own thread, so that a silvery silk-lined road is gradually built up beneath them. Fabre persuaded such a procession to climb up a large urn to its brim, which they processed around until the column met itself; he then brushed off the superfluous caterpillars and their silk track, and left the rest to their circular march, of which he spares us not a detail. Not even the pungent presence of a pine branch close to their route could deflect them from their innate propensity to follow their leader. Fabre, inexorable ringmaster, rails at them for their stupidity; he is horrified and fascinated by their blind adherence to precedent. Seven days later, having lost many members through weariness and starvation, the column eventually stumbles off the rim, and the survivors are soon feeding again.

The other unforgettable scenario concerns a moth Fabre calls the Great Peacock, which is not found in Britain. The largest of European moths, it measures 15 cm wingtip to wingtip, and has an eye-like roundel on each of its wings, to deter predators. Fabre had acquired a cocoon of this species, from which a female moth soon emerged. He kept it under a dome of wire mesh. The following night, the house was besieged by male Great Peacocks, and for some nights thereafter, in fact until the still virgin female had laid its barren eggs. A few simple experiments convinced Fabre that sight played no part in the males' wayfinding. Were they guided by a scent to which we are insensitive? If so, the large feathery antennae that distinguish the males were probably the organs involved. Fabre took a pair of scissors and snipped off the antennae of some of the male moths during their daytime somnolence; this did not seem to annoy them in the least, but the results of this experiment were statistically indeterminate. The news of the females' emergence was probably spread by some effluvium to which humans are insensitive and which he found was not masked by such strong scents as naphthalene and cigarette smoke, but he could not prove this. (Nowadays we know about pheromones, exteriorized hormones that can waft afar and excite the males' mating instincts; we know this happens in humans too.) Fabre's experience with the Great Peacock was soon repeated with a slightly smaller but closely related moth, the oak eggar. I was familiar with the handsome caterpillar of this moth, which I used to come across feeding on heather on Ilkley Moor. It grows to about three inches in length, is densely, softly furry (the golden-brown hairs can irritate the skin or eyes), with belt-like bands of black velvet. I often tried to raise them, being both fascinated and repelled by Fabre's description of the moths' flocking in at his windows, but so far as I remember none of them became female moths, and so I never managed to incite an erotic Provençal night-riot around our sober grey house in the north of England.

Reading Fabre's texts now, I am amazed at their violence. Did the kindly old curatical figure who looked over my shoulder as I scrutinized the little bees of Ilkley Moor write this account of a small *Philanthus* wasp attacking a hive-bee?

I place under the bell-glass a Philanthus and two or three hive-bees. They soon quiet down; and the spoiler begins to notice her surroundings. The antennae are pointed forwards, enquiringly; the hind-legs are drawn up with a little quiver of greed in the tarsi; the head turns to right and left and follows the evolutions of the bees against the glass. The miscreant's posture now becomes a striking piece of acting: you can read in it the fierce longings of the creature lying in ambush, the crafty waiting for the moment to commit the crime. The choice is made: the Philanthus pounces on her prey. Turn by turn tumbling over and tumbled, the two insects roll upon the ground. The tumult soon abates; and the murderess prepares to strangle her capture. The Bee is lying on her back; and the Philanthus, belly to belly with her, grips her with her six legs while snapping at her neck with her mandibles. The abdomen is now curved forward from behind, along the prostrate victim, feels with its tip, gropes about a little and ends by reaching the under part of the neck. The sting enters, lingers for a moment in the wound; and all is over. Immediately after the operation I take the Bee from the Philanthus. There are here not any of the signs of life to which I have been accustomed in my old studies of insect paralysis: the antennary threads waving slowly to and fro, the palpi quivering, the mandibles opening and closing for days, weeks and months on end. At most, the tarsi tremble for a minute or two; that constitutes the whole death-struggle. Complete immobility ensues. The inference drawn from this sudden inertia is inevitable: the Wasp has stabbed the cervical ganglia. Hence the immediate cessation of movement in all the organs of the head; hence the real instead of the apparent death of the Bee. The Philanthus is a butcher and not a paralyser.

The prose is as ruthless as the procedures observed; Fabre's interventions, as with the exhausted caterpillars or the moths with amputated antennae, are equally callous. But behind the implacably objective observer driven by the compulsion to know is Fabre the sun-worshipper, who made his foundational experiment as a child:

There I stand one day, a pensive urchin, with my hands behind my back and my face turned to the sun. The dazzling splendour fascinates me. I am the Moth attracted by the light of the lamp. With what am I enjoying the glorious radiance: with my mouth or my eyes? That is the question put by my budding scientific curiosity. Reader, do not smile: the future observer is already practising and experimenting. I open my mouth wide and close my eyes: the glory disappears. I open my eyes and shut my mouth: the glory reappears. I repeat the performance, with the same result. The question's solved: I have learnt by deduction that I see the sun with my eyes.

But the sun pours darkness into the world as well as light, driving the circuitry of life far from equilibrium, through states of bliss and agony that make our groping ideas of good and evil seem a parochial concern. Fabre tells us the truth of the matter, as the cicada sings it.

Contrescarpe

Albertine, of 'Hispano-Sarrasin blood', born and abandoned 1937, Algiers; adopted and taken to Aix-en-Provence by an elderly French family who found her uncontrollable; raped by her adoptive uncle, arrested for *'vagabondage'*, placed by her family in a reformatory; escaped to Paris, lived by theft and prostitution; visited her father and stole his pistol; arrested in the course of armed robbery, sent to Fresnes Prison; showed herself to be a gifted student but a recalcitrant prisoner with an unquenchable resentment of authority; escaped at night by jumping from a high wall, breaking her ankle bone or *astragale,* crawled half naked and in agony to the nearby highway, was scooped up by a motorcyclist: *An arm encircled my shoulders, another slipped under my knees; I was lifted, carried off; he carried me securely and gently, I had left the mud and I walked, in his arms, between heaven and earth.* Her saviour was Julien Sarrazin, born 1924, Feuquières, near Amiens, seventh of his violent, alcoholic criminal father's twelve children; the family's main food-gatherer during the Occupation, arrested 1943 with his younger brother George for robbing trains bound for Germany; condemned to fifteen years hard labour, participated in the prison revolt of Melun in 1944 and tried to escape with George, who was shot dead by the Germans. Recaptured, released in 1953; continued to live by crime; found Albertine, hid her in his mother's house; both of them repeatedly drawn to robbery, and it was in jail that they married and Albertine wrote the autobiographical novel, *L'Astragale* (1965), that made her famous and notorious. At the end of her book, shortly after Julien has been released from prison, Albertine is rearrested. She accepts her fate with a smile: *We will meet again on the luminous platform. Once more, one of us is at the foot of the slope. Turn by turn we must clamber and haul.* And it seems they did attain to that sunlit height. A grateful former client of Albertine's bought them an old farm near Montpellier. Photographs from this last period show her delicate but rebellious little face and Julien's tender watch over her; the impression is of a golden time, but it was brief. Her health was ruinous and in 1967, aged 29, she died from a botched kidney operation. Julien pursued those responsible through the legal system; they were condemned to short prison terms and Julien was awarded damages of 40,000 francs in 'exact reparation for the loss of his wife'.

In 2011 M and I stayed for some months in the Centre Culturel Irlandais in Paris, near Place de la Contrescarpe, which I passed through almost every day. The name interested me, and when I found a grubby old paperback entitled *Contrescarpe* in one of the heaped trays outside a bookshop in the Rue des Écoles, I snatched it up. To my surprise it turned out to be the autobiography of Julien Sarrazin, and it is a vigorous, slangy, passionate work, a worthy response to *L'Astragale,* which Albertine called her 'little love-story for Julien'. It ends with his finding of the girl dropped out of the sky: *After that my sole concern was to hide and care for the kid. Her injury was very serious, nursing took up months and months, but I had found a reason for living, a precious and savage reason. I felt myself responsible, without analysis. What ought to be done, must be done.*

Contrescarpe appeared in 1974 and is long out of print. The word does not occur in Julien's book, I found, but an introductory note mentions this mysterious title and suggests that it is easier to fall down the *contrescarpe* of life than to climb up it. An archaeologist friend met in Paris told me that it is a term of fortification: the inner wall or slope of a defensive ditch is the *scarpe* and the outer one the *contrescarpe.* He also pointed out a plaque in the Rue Descartes, which slopes down northwards from Place de la Contrescarpe, indicating the position of a long-vanished gate of the wall built by Philip II Augustus in 1200–1215 to protect the city against the Anglo-Norman Plantagenets while he was away on the Third Crusade. In the fourteenth century this wall was strengthened by digging a large ditch in front of it and heaping the spoil against the inside of the wall. Craggy lengths and cross-sections of the wall show up here and there among the smooth-plastered façades lining Rue Descartes, but the ditch and its outer slope that gave the little square its name have long been levelled out of existence.

In 1955 the psychogeographer Guy Debord, who was shortly to found the Situationist International, wrote: *It has long been said that the desert is monotheistic. Is it illogical or devoid of interest to observe that the district in Paris between Place de la Contrescarpe and Rue de l'Arbalète conduces rather to atheism, to oblivion and to the disorientation of habitual reflexes?* One can only answer such a query by imagined revisitings. Place de la Contrescarpe is small and fre-quently crowded. On three of its sides are restaurants and bars fronted by ranks of little chairs and tables on the pavements, under red canopies. The centre of the Place is marked by a small fountain surrounded by a rather sparse grove of young trees, within a circle of cast-iron posts linked by loops of chain. The space immediately within the chained circle is the preserve of two street-dwellers, stubby men wearing layers of clothing made grey by weather. One of them has his hair in dread-locks. They lie stretched out on bits of cardboard, or on the bare cobbles. Occasionally they exchange a few brief curses but otherwise seem to have little to do with each other. My passing glimpses of their tedious and com-fortless existences tell me little about how they live, where they find food, where they spend their nights. It does not seem that God tempers the wind to them. There is also an elderly lady in a long greyish overcoat who circulates in the square accosting passers-by. Her speech is a shouted whisper like a sudden venting of compressed air. Once she materialized unnoticed behind M and addressed her with an explosive hiss of 'Madame!' that startled her into jumping from one side of me to the other as if fleeing a curse – a most inhabitual reflex for M, normally so open-hearted.

Five narrow streets diverge from the Place, two of them climbing northwards and westwards, two falling eastwards towards the Jardin des Plantes, and the other, Rue Mouffetard, dropping steeply away to the south. This street is the spine of the area indicated by Debord. It is narrow, cobbled and picturesque, but not too selfconsciously so. There are queues outside certain pâtisseries, dashing young men preside over their smoking hotplates in crêperies no bigger than cupboards, the jewellers' displays and the vegetable stalls are exquisitely colour-coordinated, scores of identical cane chairs press together as closely as possible outside restaurants around corners off the street. In the Christmas season countless tiny lights form a web suspended above the street from end to end that might have been scissored out of the Milky Way. Among the branches of the trees in the Place more lights cleverly imitate the soft fall of big snowflakes. Everything is enchanted; even one of the street-dwellers lying by the fountain as if fallen to the very foot of the contrescarpe of life, oblivious to the busy shoppers stepping around and over him, is parcelled up in silver foil, a Christmas present nobody wants.

Byzantium

Byzantium exists

'Dogs bark; the caravan moves on' – an ancient saying a Turkish friend taught me in its most condensed form: *it ürür, kervan yürür.* Whatever the plaints and scoffs of the shallow and uninformed, Byzantium has outlived history itself and will haunt us forever. My first glimpse of its ghost was in 1958 as I was puzzling my way through the clamorous chaos of Istanbul to a youth hostel from the ferry that had brought me from Athens. Sunset was strewing the dark caverns of the little side streets with gold dust. How did I come to associate this glimmering in the air with Byzantium? Only a few days earlier on some Aegean island I had overheard the term 'Byzantium', which to my eager ears crackled with exoticism, in a conversation between two of my elders. Such was my ignorance that I did not know whether they were talking about a city (which they were: Constantinople, the Greek Orthodox precursor of Muslim Istanbul), an empire (that too: the Byzantine Empire, originally the eastern wing of the Roman Empire), or a style (most especially this: a whole civilization in fact, its greatest monument the Church of the Holy Wisdom, Hagia Sophia, in Istanbul, its visual art that of the icon, its bureaucracy a byword for impenetrable complexity). A year later, returning to Istanbul with M to take up a teaching post in Robert Academy on the Bosphorus a few miles north of the city, I found we were living almost in the shadow of Rumeli Hisar, 'the fortress on the land of the Romans', built by the Ottoman Turks in preparation for the siege and capture of Constantinople in 1453. The balcony of our apartment gave us a lofty view of the further, Asiatic, shore of the Bosphorus and the towers of Anadolu Hisar, 'the fortress of Anatolia', the counterpart of Rumeli Hisar. Thus the defeated 'land of the Romans' became part of our address.

The school I was preaching mathematics in prepares students for Robert College, originally a nineteenth-century missionary endeavour but long identified with the secular, modernizing Turkey founded by Atatürk; it has since become the University of the Bosphorus. But the old Ottoman world lay all about it. Our house was on a steep twisty cobbled lane called Fenerli Turbe Yolü, 'the street of the lantern-lit tomb', so called from a low, stone-built vault, the tomb of a Dervish saint, a few hundred yards further up. Tied to the bars of a window-like recess in the tomb were little scraps of paper on which suppliants had written prayers. Some of them were from students of mine: 'May I pass my exam this year,' for example. A few miles down the Bosphorus is the village of Tarabya, which I have read is so called from the Turkish for 'pleasure', a name bestowed on it by a sultan who enjoyed a fish meal here, or from the Greek *therapia*, for its curative airs and health-giving springs. But I have been told that these stories are false; that the sorceress Medea, sailing down the Bosphorus with Jason and the Argonauts after they had stolen the Golden Fleece, scattered poison on the shore here, and that the place was later named Therapia to undo the consequent curse on it. The world of ancient myth is deeply scored into the land here, most notably in the shape of the Bosphorus itself, the magnificent straits connecting the Sea of Marmara to the Black Sea and separating Asia from Europe. This, according to Time's amateur etymology, is the 'cattle-passage', crossed by the nymph Io, who had been changed into a beautiful heifer by Zeus to cover up one of his affairs and was condemned by his jealous wife Juno to wander the earth plagued by a gadfly. Nearby is the site of a pillar on the top of which a saint, imitating the famous St Simeon Stylites of Syria, spent his days and nights in suffering and prayer. Perhaps this high-perched personage can see through the mythical, classical and Ottoman centuries for me and deep into the atmosphere of Byzantium. On blazing summer days the sky must have been to him like the background of an icon, of solid gold hammered as thin as salamander skin. In winter the vicious Kara Yel, the 'black wind' from the north, would occasionally have plastered him with dust swept up from the Steppes, rendering him as hard to read from ground level as a marginal figure in a gravy-splashed icon in some ancient monastic refectory.

The Tessera

I was in Hagia Sophia one day, trying to make out the devil's face that according to my Turkish friend had recently been discerned in the symmetrically patterned wall-panelling of sliced and unfolded marble. Out of the vague hush of visitors adrift in the vast spaces of the ancient cathedral, a tiny but precise sound at my feet made me look down. A glinting object lay before me, the size of my middle fingernail. I stooped for it. It was a fragment of plaster, coloured as if dipped in burnt honey and bearing a scrap of gold leaf. Evidently it had fallen from one of the mosaics of the domed ceiling floating far above me. Perhaps, after many a loosening shock, it had been finally dislodged by an earth tremor too slight to be noticeable in earthquake-prone Turkey; I have read that earthquakes have cracked the dome and even brought it crashing down several times during the long centuries of the building's history. The mosaic of Christ Pantocrator that once looked down from the centre of the dome was painted over with a vortex of Islamic calligraphy centuries ago when the building was in use as a mosque, after the Ottoman conquest of Byzantium. Today, studying reproductions of the remaining mosaics, and trying to remember where I stood at the time, I conclude that the fallen tessera formed part of one of the four huge 'hexapteryga' or six-winged cherubim who seem effortlessly, by prayer alone, to hold the mighty dome aloft between them. I have it still, kept in a matchbox, more than fifty years after its entry into my life. It was not a message, but the significances I invest it with demand decryption.

Athenagoras

Nowadays Hagia Sophia is a museum, but might, the way things are going, become a mosque again. Byzantium, though, still shows through modern Turkey. M and I once attended an Easter Sunday service in the cathedral of the Patriarchate of Constantinople, accompanied and guided by a Greek student of mine, an insufferable know-all nicknamed Aristotle. From our toehold in a balcony crammed with worshippers, of whom according to Aristotle seventy-three busloads had come from Greece for the occasion, it was difficult to see the gilded, incense-fuming, lava-like flow of the proceedings below.

Towards the end of the ceremony, representatives of various faiths gave brief readings each in their own language, and Aristotle took it upon himself to inform us, and those standing around us, what these languages were. I was delighted when a ringing Anglican voice struck up a cheerful and a godly note with 'And on the Third Day . . .', and Aristotle turned to me and whispered, 'Armenian, sir.' The Patriarch himself, Athenagoras, stood out from the throng of splendidly robed and high-hatted clerics, whom he overtopped by a head and a hat. Later we were to meet this imposing figure face to face – a solemn occasion that threatened to descend into farce.

One day Aristotle proposed guiding an English colleague of mine, Geoffrey, and myself on a visit to Mount Athos, the reclusive peninsula of northern Greece whose dense forests, steep slopes and gynophobic ordinances shelter twenty ancient Orthodox monasteries from the pollution of the female. Aristotle announced that we would need a document of permission from the Patriarchate, where, fortunately, he himself was well received and could facilitate our request. On the appointed day Aristotle collected Geoff, M and myself in his enormous and powerful car, and roared off with us to Fener, the quietly decaying neighbourhood of Istanbul in which the patriarchal cathedral and the Patriarch's residence face each other across a courtyard flower garden. But first, Aristotle advised, we should buy the Patriarch a present. What sort of present would be suitable for a Patriarch, we asked; flowers, perhaps? Chocolates, or Metaxas brandy, prescribed Aristotle. We diverted to the most fashionable sweetshop in the city, where he demanded, on our behalf, the most enormous box of chocolates I have ever seen; it must have been three feet square at least. And on our return from Athos, he advised, we should bring the Patriarchate some choice wine.

At the Patriarchate we languished for a while in a sequence of dingy offices, where our massive gift was whisked away by silent young monks. Then Geoff, M and I were led into the presence. Athenagoras, a majestic figure with craggy brow, arched nose and streaming white beard, patted us into place on a row of hard little chairs facing his big desk. Was this a foretaste of the Last Judgement? I noted a photograph of President Truman on the desk, and a row of books, their spines presented to us: three volumes of Truman's autobiography, and a set of ten little works on Mental Efficiency. Athenagoras hooded his fierce black eyes and pronounced, 'You are from Robert College. I visited the College, just fifty-six years ago.' We were silent. My eye fell on the title of the first volume on Mental Efficiency: *Timidity, how to overcome it.* But it seemed we were there, not to speak, but to receive a series of rounded utterances on 'furthering the cause of Enlightenment, Westernization, the Liberal Mind, and of course [long pause . . .] Education'.

A junior cleric appeared bearing three little glasses of water and a bowl of something sticky and white. What new social ordeal was this? *Poise, how to obtain it,* was the title of another of the little volumes before us. M was the first to dig a spoon into the bowl, and then couldn't get it out. His Holiness was kind enough to disengage it for her, saying with what might have been a malicious grin buried in his beard, 'An oriental custom!' He continued his monologue. Yes, America had left forever her native shores; where was she now? She was here, and in the Far East, and in Africa, fighting the world's battles, spreading lofty ideals . . . And then, to M, 'And where were you born? Ireland? An island near Britain. You are not American! And you? England! And you? Also England!' This caused a brief hiatus; I wondered if he might summon an underling to remove Truman and Mental Efficiency and replace them, say, with Churchill and the *Golden Treasury,* but he recovered himself magnificently. 'But what would America be, without her mother country? What a power for good your Empire has been! The Pax Britannica! What have they gained, those countries who have left the fold? Was it really worth the struggle, the loss of life, this so-called liberty? India, Malaya, Ghana . . .' The awkward subject of Cyprus loomed. 'Cyprus! That was very unfortunate, it should not have happened, all that trouble between Greece and Britain. And Greece and Turkey!' We relaxed as the corner was turned.

'Well, that's enough politics! And where are you going this summer? Mount Athos! Well now . . .' I fixed my eye on the next volume of the set: *Influence, and how to exert it,* and ventured, 'We wondered if you could . . .' And then it seemed the audience was over. Athenagoras rose to usher us out. He took M's hand and gazed deep into her eyes. 'You are so nice. And to what church do you belong?' and when M confessed she belonged to no church, 'How can you? You *must*!' Then, assuming that he was M's unfortunate husband, he put an immense arm around Geoff's shoulders, almost smothering him in the Patriarchal beard, and planted a long sympathetic kiss on the top of his head, pinioning M with his other hand the meanwhile. To me he gave only a handshake and a reproving look; he had caught me smirking at his self-help books.

Mount Athos

Before we left the Patriarchate's offices we composed a flowery petition for permission to visit the holy monasteries of Mount Athos for the purpose of veneration and study, and were eventually issued with an impressive document. In the following summer vacation Aristotle, Geoff and I travelled to Thessaloniki in northern Greece, where we applied for permission from the police to visit Athos; this took all day as we were batted around from office to office, and our cherished letter from the Patriarchate seemed to arouse more ill-will than respect. In the end Aristotle was refused permission on the grounds that he might be trying to evade conscription, and had to return to Istanbul; we said goodbye to him with relief.

There are no roads into Athos, so we took a little ferry from the port of Larissa along the eastern shores of the peninsula to the monastery of Vatopedi, where we spent the night, and the next morning we laboured uphill on a knobbly forest path to Karyes, the capital: a tiny village of slate-roofed houses enjoying a siesta under their broad eaves, and little shops selling crude wooden spoons and suchlike from the various monasteries. There we presented our permit to the religious authorities. To our surprise it was dismissed with an obscene gesture; Athos, we learned, was resentful of Patriarchal authority. The next day we hired a mule and a muleteer, and set off downhill to visit one of the monasteries on the eastern shore; I rode the mule, which was adept at walking with its feet in single file among the tangled tree-roots, while Geoffrey strode out with a huge stick. On the way we passed a prelate in magnificent silken robes walking through the woods accompanied by two handsome youths in clerical garb, who disconcertingly batted their long curved eyelashes at us; they led us through vineyards and orchards to a little ecclesiastical foundation of some kind where a young monk served us ouzo and figs in the porch. Ouzo, we learned, protects against syphilis and cancer; if so, to judge by the amount of ouzo we were offered in our travels, those ills must be unknown on the holy mountain.

Rejoining our route, we reached the great monastery of Iveron in the late afternoon. Its grim walls rose to forty feet or so before being broken by windows and balconies. We had arrived on the second day of a three-day feast, and some monks and muleteers were lying on the grass outside the entrance, sunning themselves in a headachy way. They greeted us, and two of them led us in to show us to the guest quarters. Recruitment to the monastic life had so fallen off at that time, a low point in the history of the holy mountain, that some of the monasteries were deserted and others half empty. Here, we learned, the monks now had two or three cells each. More ouzo was produced; in one cell I noted pin-up magazines on a table. The monks were a gamesome crew. As they conducted us back along a dark corridor I noticed that Geoff, by my side, was hurrying along in a peculiar manner, raising his knees very high; he later told me that one of the monks had pinched his bottom.

That evening we joined some two hundred monks, muleteers and other servants, and a few visitors, around a horseshoe of tables in the great refectory. There were blackish icons on the wall behind us, and the air was full of the crackling of countless candles. Opposite me was a merry white-bearded father, whom we were told was a Spanish prince. A fearsome stooping hermit grinned at me hairily as he swept a horrible mess of fish-heads and melon skins into a sack to take home to his cell on the hillside above. After the meal we were entertained with chanting by a delegation of monks from another monastery, which we applauded by tapping our wine tumblers with our forks; the succession of songs seemed endless, although the Spanish prince tried to hurry it along by beating his tumbler long before the end of each offering. A dead-drunk muleteer had to be carried out between two of his comrades. When we emerged into the dark central courtyard, the monks scattered and furtively lit up cigarettes, and the Master of Ceremonies rushed around trying to suppress this. One monk went off with a young German tourist. Somebody was being sick on a balcony far above.

A day or two later, by which time we had reached the little port of Daphni on the western shore of the peninsula, I decided to visit the famous monastery of Simonopetra, a few miles to the south; Geoff, more of a socialite than I, opted instead to accept an invitation to lunch on board a smart-looking yacht moored in the bay. A little ferryboat took me along the coast below crags and precipitous forest slopes. As it came into view, the gravity-defying stance of the monastery on a vast ragged pyramid of rock took my breath away. The façades of its main buildings – great keep-like towers with balconies across four or five of their upper storeys — seemed to be rooted in a vertical cliff face and supported by pinnacles of rock that clambered up and clasped the lower storeys. A steep cobbled tunnel hewn through the rock linked the little quay below with the courtyard above; mules trotted down it with a clatter that might have been an echo from medieval centuries.

There were very few monks in Simonopetra at that period. One of them greeted me, the only visitor, and showed me around. He explained that whereas many of the monastic communities were 'cenobitic', that is, the monks ate and worshipped communally, this one was 'idiorrhythmic', each monk ordering his own life of prayer, meditation, work and refection. Then I went back down the tunnel to stand on the little quay and marvel at the eagle-like perch of the monastery far above me. A monk appeared on one of the highest balconies; on spotting me below he whisked back into his cell and reappeared with binoculars. I dodged into the shelter of the tunnel and after a while made my way up to the courtyard again. But there he was, posing in a little doorway with his hip stuck out like a prostitute. Disconcerted, I decided I'd had enough of the idiorrhythmic, and would return to Daphni and thence sail away from the holy mountain. Since there would be no ferry at that hour I set off to walk over the stony scrub-grown hills, where I got stuck in a thornbush and extricated myself only with difficulty.

Many years later, at dinner in an artists' centre in Ireland, I found myself seated opposite an elderly and eminent Greek poet. The centre, I suppose one could say, was cenobitic with pronounced idiorrhythmic tendencies, and lively dinner-table talk was prized. When the subject of Mount Athos came up I was about to launch into a well-polished anecdote of my serio-comic experiences there when I realized that our guest had a profound veneration for the place, and so I held my peace.

I believe I was right to censor myself so. Common respect for others' freedom of opinion, especially in a setting of comradeship, told me not to thrust my anticlericalism and atheism down the poet's throat at the dining table. Nevertheless I believe that any important belief system should be submitted to trial by laughter from time to time. If faith is belief without evidence, it is foolishness, no matter if Hagia Sophia itself is founded on it. I treasure my own share of absurdities and admit to resting on certain beliefs that my powers of reason have not quite dared test to destruction. Here, for instance, is my rough and ready argument against supernaturalism, by which I mean belief in nonmaterial beings, life after death, etc.

Knowing little about it, I like to imagine that the classical orchestra is the outcome of the joint evolution of the instruments comprising it; I imagine for instance that the piccolo, flute, clarinet etc. are the survivors of many rivalrous types of wind instrument each claiming territory in a space with dimensions of pitch, timbre and other musical qualities. If I am right, the components of the orchestra have, over the centuries of rubbing shoulders, distinguished themselves one from the other to make their contributions the better jointly to cover the field of sound in which the orchestra can range. And so it is with the many organelles that play their parts in the little orchestra of the biological cell. Now that scientists can see deep into microspace we know that every cell, whether of amoeba, oak or human neighbour, contains a set of complex and delicate structures that act in coordination to effect the cell's functioning and replication. Also it seems that some of these interior organs of the cell originated as viruses or bacteria, which found a congenial environment in the cell and survived because they supplied some need in its economy. Thus by a slow-acting law of Darwinian selection – to survive, contribute to the survival of your environment – these heterogeneous contraptions have come into cooperative existence: an orchestra, far from note-perfect, bearing traces of its higgledy-piggledy origins, but of wondrous performative powers. I'll look at the chromosome, a part of the chief of these curious instruments, the nucleus.

A chromosome is a threadlike molecule of DNA

normally wound around a number of spool-like structures of protein. The DNA molecule consists of two strands spiralling around each other. Each strand is a chain of units composed of a sugar, a phosphate, and a molecular structure called a base. The sugar of one unit combines with the phosphate of the next, so creating a tough backbone, to which the bases are attached. Bases are of four kinds, the names of which are abbreviated as C, G, A and T. Because of their different shapes, an A on one strand of the chromosome fits together with a T on the other strand, while a C fits together with a G. Genes are segments of the sequence of such base pairs along a chromosome, and the totality of these sequences constitutes the genome. In a human cell there are about 3.2 billion base pairs; in a simple plant cell there are about 127 million. These matters are central to the question of what life is and how it transmits itself from generation to generation; the sequences of bases constituting the genes encode the instructions for the building of different proteins from simpler chemicals, and it is the proteins that carry out the functions of the cells. All this is only the crudest sketch of the chromosome, a mere mention of its constructive capabilities; I have said nothing of its capacity for self-duplication. Other cellular machines, such as that by which the genetic code is read and the necessary ingredients located and delivered to the sites at which the various proteins are compounded, are at least as wonderfully odd.

However, all this material bricolage is completely superfluous. The disembodied soul can do as much, and much more, without proteins or DNA. Christ Pantocrator can bring persons into and out of existence without the crazy contraptions of the cell, the aeons of evolution necessary to concoct which were a waste of time. Hence the futility of fleshly existence, this tedious tale of chemical imbecility.

Of course that last paragraph is written in order to awake a protest. Surely the existence of a chemical complex that lives and dies, that can pass on its characteristics to its offspring, that knows something of its own structure and even entertains hopes of penetrating that ultimate mystery of physiology, the brain's enactment of mentality, is a marvel that eclipses all transcendentalism. The domes of our skulls need no hexapteryga to hold them aloft; the devil is not hidden in the patterns of our neurons; the fallen tessera bears what message I choose to send from self to self; supernaturalism is blasphemy.

The Centre of Gravity:
two incidents joined by a note

Something was wrong; I knew it as soon as I woke. I was where I was supposed to be – in one of the beds of a six-bed dormitory on an RAF station in Malaya – but of the clothing I had worn the previous evening, and which normally would be strewn on the foot of the bed or hung over the back of a chair beside it, not an item was to be seen. For a few minutes I could not make sense of this situation. Then a blissful memory gradually condensed, purely tactile at first, in my skin rather than in my mind: the touch of cool air on my naked body as I strolled by moonlight among soaring palm trees. But where had I shed my status in the world of the dressed, my externalized social centre of gravity? I wrapped a towel around me and, as if following the spoor of a dream, retraced the hundred yards or so from the cluster of dormitories to the washroom block. There I found my clothes, neatly piled in the corner of a shower cubicle.

My room-mates had long been trying to persuade me to join them on one of their forays to Pleasure Island, a short ferry ride from a little jetty a mile or two from the station. What mattered to me of this island were the butterfly-haunted walks on the flanks of its central, jungle-clad hill, and the meditative calm of the Million Buddhas Precious Pagoda in the garden of its chief temple. I knew its port town only as a few streets of little open-fronted shops exhibiting gorgeous drifts of shapes and colours. Behind these shops I knew was another realm, a seething complexity of dwellings, bars, sweat-shops churning out that avalanche of forms, temples of at least four faiths, and brothels of none. Along the shoreline and encroaching on tidal flats were the poorest houses, ragged birds' nests tottering on stilts over black mud. The Military Police made occasional sweeps through this agglomeration of humanity, parts of which were out of bounds to us because of the activities of Chinese Triad gangs and of communist terrorists. Nevertheless one of our number was reputed to know this labyrinth intimately and was well enough received there to be let dodge from house to house and so evade the MPs. He was in thrall to one of the lovely girls with whom this human coral reef was bejewelled; she was an immigrant from Siam, and was feared as a witch by her Chinese neighbours. Also she was said to be a prostitute, as some of his unfeeling mates liked to remind him; but he never accepted this.

Although I was fascinated by the thought of this secretive quarter and aching with adolescent desire for its exotic girls, my entrenched inhibitions, shyness and cowardice had so far kept me out of it. But it seemed unjust to me, who regarded myself as the artist, the bohemian, the adventurer and romantic of the radar workshops, that one of my comrades, and he the most prosaic and unimaginative of us all, was having a passionate love affair with a Siamese witch while I was spending lonely hours in the camp's sterile cafeteria. And so, the evening before the awakening described above, I had let myself be carried along with the gang, whose prescription for my troubles was drink, drink, drink.

There are a few narrow windows in the wall of forgetfulness surrounding that night. Since I disliked beer and whisky I probably drank a lot of sticky-sweet liqueurs. I remember swaying as if my centre of gravity was orbiting like a moth around a light, while I raised a glass in a bar, empty but for one of my comrades who had stayed to watch over me when the others had disappeared into the unknown, and three Chinese barmen observing me with deferential smiles. And then I was on the phone to the station guardhouse, swearing that I was someone else and another someone else was doing my guard duty for me that night, until my mate poured a drink into the telephone and I was cut off. Finally a glass of brandy knocked me stony sober in a dancehall called the City Lights, leaving me on a gloomy island in a sea of hilarity, so that I saw what a horrible place it was, like a huge dark derelict railway station with vaguely indecent paintings on the walls and a raucous band far away, a dense throng of Chinese, Malays, Indians and whites dancing, and a few servicemen propped semiconscious on the tables. Then I was marshalling a group of my friends into trishaws, dissuading them from visiting the brothels, and racing through the silent streets to catch the last ferry, at half past one, to the mainland.

Something rather incomprehensible happened on that ferry. I was slumped on a bench on deck, half asleep and trying to remain unconscious of the reeling rout packing the deck around me, when I became aware of a persistent annoyance: a face thrust near mine and bellowing at me. It was that of a loutish fellow from the camp who spent his days insulting all who came near him. When I think of him now I realize that he must have been mentally disturbed, but I did not understand this at the time; in fact I had already made up my mind that I was going to challenge and fight him the very next time our paths crossed. This rather public-schoolboy determination is so far from my nature that I am sure I would have somehow evaded my commitment; however, as it happened (and I do not know how it happened), the occasion never arose. As the irritating growling and yelping continued I slid down on my bench, brought one knee up to my chest, planted my foot against my tormentor's pulpy ton-weight centre of gravity, and, without troubling to wake up any further, vigorously straightened my leg. The ugly face was withdrawn and disappeared with satisfying finality.

It is surely a mere coincidence that I never saw the man again. We were a shifting, rootless society; people were posted to other camps for no known reason, repatriated for discharge, or sent off to a hill station for rest and recuperation, sometimes at very short notice. I never enquired after him. I like to think he is in orbit still.

Associated with any object having weight is a point, called its centre of gravity, such that the object responds to any external force as if all its weight were concentrated at that point. (I glide over technical distinctions between weight and mass, centre of mass and centre of gravity, as they are irrelevant to considerations of bodies – such as ours – in the almost uniform gravitational field obtaining near and on the earth's surface.) Thus my own centre of gravity can be seen as the nexus between my materiality and that of the rest of the universe, the umbilicus of my gravitational being. Body parts that have achieved iconic status include the brow (the Enlightenment thinker lets his head fall forward as if weighted down by its contents, and buttresses his forehead with his knuckles), the heart (in the days of sensibility orators would signal their sincerity by clapping right hand to left chest), the loins as the ageless seat of desire (rock-star sex-deities propose the groin for ritualized lust). Today a purely conceptual point should be added to the list, the centre of gravity, the bearer of the truth that we are wholly and without surplus parts of the material world.

I say 'purely conceptual' because an object's centre of gravity does not always lie within the substance of the object. For instance the centre of gravity of a bowl is in its hollow, while that of a double star is somewhere between its two components, and nearer to the heavier; both revolve about it, but it may not lie within either. The centre of gravity of a high-jumper's body follows a trajectory determined by its weight and the force imparted by the legs at take-off, which the jumper tries to maximize – and then by arching the body like a horseshoe he or she can get each part of it in turn over the bar while the centre of gravity passes beneath it, thus stealing another couple of inches of height above what seems possible. In fact any mobile human body's centre of gravity is in perpetual negotiation with the external world; it is a coin spent and recuperated, the price and profit of passage through space.

Can one ever lose one's centre of gravity? In metaphor, perhaps; in the fantasy of the spiritual, of being rid of the ball-and-chain of embodiment. Not in dreams though, if mine are anything to go by, being all too often of precarious flight over horrid depths or slipping and overbalancing on the verge of precipices. And certainly not in reality, not even in the experience of weightlessness, in which one's physical response to non-gravitational forces is still ordered by the centre of gravity. However, there is a slight incident that in long-distance memory feels like an instance of loss of the centre of gravity. Like the drunken episode described above, it answers to the recall of my youthful sojourn in Malaya.

Left to my own purposes in the camp I soon discovered a little theatrical society that spanned the straits between service personnel and the intellectual elite of Pleasure Island. This sybaritic group never got around to putting on a performance, but in the processes of choosing a play, designing the setting, reading and rehearsing, it provided amusement to its members. That at least is how it seemed to me, ignorant of the secretive politics that agitated one or two radical young Chinese members of the society and were perhaps discussed only in private by their seniors. Our mentor was a cultivated expatriate school headmaster who, with his wife, entertained us bountifully on their airy, shaded, verandas. Two or three technicians of the same lowly status as myself, undergoing National Service before entering university; Mike, an anarchical intelligence officer who abused his rank to liberate me from the tedium of the radar workshop by sending for me to undertake urgent missions, such as translating some bit of French pornography I found as baffling as he did; a rubber planter deeply versed in Britishness; the beautiful Bee, an Asian Audrey Hepburn; Mavis, of some lovely concoction of races but convicted of seriousness, having been caught reading a British Council pamphlet on Milton during a picnic . . . such were my new soul companions.

Picnics were the essence of our lifestyle. Shaded by the coconut palms that leaned protectively out over the broiling beaches and womb-warm coastal waters, we lolled and laughed; I probably held forth, more than was appropriate for one so inexperienced, on the tumult of ideas fermenting in my head. I had a theory of God as a construction out of the immediate data of mystical experience, which lost us many a half hour; also a demolition of the concept of free will, which one day we decided to put to the test by making no decisions at all. Mike and I were swimming when this experiment was to begin; we soon found ourselves adrift in a gentle longshore current, which seemed perfectly apropos. We had perhaps taken a glass of wine. As the dark-green wall of close-packed vegetation behind the beach glided effortlessly by we intoned a favourite poem of our sect, Thomas Love Peacock's grown-up rendering of the old nursery rhyme about going to sea in a bowl:

> Fear ye not the waves that roll?
> No, in charmèd bowl we swim.
> What the charm that floats the bowl?
> Water may not pass the brim.
> The bowl goes trim. The moon doth shine,
> And our ballast is old wine.

. . . and we droned and drew out the refrain in hollow tones, again and again: 'And our ballast is old wine . . .'

Nothing went wrong; we were not swept out to sea and thrown ashore on a desert island, or snapped up by sharks. Simply, we remembered that the distance we had travelled was real, and that we would have to walk back – that is, our centres of gravity, our wills and weights, had been shipped along with us in the bowl of tipsiness. So we struck out for the land, abandoning the search for an experimental proof of my theory of free will, whatever it was.

The Gods of the Neale

For reasons not worth rehearsing, when I set out to begin my map of Connemara, in 1979, it was from the humdrum little town of Claremorris in the flatlands of south Mayo. Slightly nervously I wheeled my overladen bike out into the busy street and wobbled off in the direction of the mountains that formed a long rim to the western horizon. The day was perfect April, compounded of sun and breeze; the roads were almost empty of traffic, the countryside very quiet. As I approached the village called The Neale I noticed a small pyramid or ziggurat of nine stages in a field by the road, and went to look at it. A largely illegible inscription seemed to identify it as 'Templum Fortunae' and date it to 1750 or 1760. Back on the road, I overtook a lady walking between two sticks, who told me that she was paralysed on one side after a brain haemorrhage. I asked her about the monument, and she was very informative. Lord Kilmaine, she said, had been one of the good landlords, and had employed the farmers ('such as they were') on building this folly as well as a small round Greek temple visible in the distance. I should go and see 'The Gods of the Neale', since I was interested in things like that. She could not explain what these Gods were, but I would find them, she said, by taking a turning to the left just ahead.

The turning sent me down a little road with a tall demesne wall along its left-hand side, overtopped by old trees. Unable to identify anything that might be a god or gods, I spoke to some children playing football in a little schoolyard on the right, who directed me onwards to a hole in the wall, which I was able to jump through. I spent some time wandering around the low remains of the mansion, tumbledown outhouses and overgrown gardens, and finally came across a monument, perhaps ten or twelve feet tall, set against a thicketed bank. Three medieval-looking rectangular bas-reliefs were inserted in its frontage; the lowest of them, horizontal, represented a slender four-footed creature, a lion to judge by its curly mane and fierce claws, with a long whip-like tail ending in what looked like a hand of three fingers and a thumb. Above that the other slabs stood vertically and side by side: on the right, an angel in a long dress, facing forwards and holding a small shield or perhaps a book against its breast; on the left a horse, perhaps a unicorn, which appeared to be sitting on its tail and looked to me as if it should have been set horizontally. Below these carvings was a broad limestone plaque with a long inscription of an eighteenth-century appearance, which in this shadowy retreat was hard to make sense of. Some phrases stood out that were given resonance by the obscurities in which they were embedded and the empty-echoing mansion nearby:

The Irish characters on the above stone import that in this cave we have by us the Gods of Cons . . . Lett us follow their stepps sick of love with FVLL confidence in Loo Lave Adda . . . the Shepherd of Ireland of his era . . . These images were found in a cave behind the place they now stand & were the ancient Gods of the Neale which took its name from them. They were called Déithe Fhéile or the Gods of Felicity from which the place in Irish is called Ne Heale in English The Neale LL reigned AM 2577 PD 927 AHTE C1496 and was then 60: CEDNA reigned AM 2994 & 64 of Edna was wel 50 CON MOIL was ye son of Heber who divided this kingdom with his brother and had the western parts of this island for his lott all which was originally called from Con Conovcht or Cons portion and his son LOO LAVE ADDA who found the Druids was thought to have drawn all his knowledge from the SVN Thus the Irish history.

N.B. the smaller letters on the upper part of the great plinth import that it was erected by Edna Loos Gods were adopted by Con and Edna of the line of Heber established their worship there 1753.

Whether myth is the consolidated sediment fallen out from the ceaseless perturbed flow of folk tales, or folk tales the crumbled remains of forgotten myth, scholarship conditions us to prefer deeper layers to later ones. So, to clear away some of the misidentifications of earlier misidentifications, I add here my findings, fruit of subsequent rummaging in archives and reference books.

Con is clearly Conn of the Hundred Battles, the king who divided Ireland with Eoghan Mór (not his brother), and took as his portion the part known from him as Connacht. Heber is probably Éibhear, the mythical leader of the Gaels, who ruled over the southern portion of Ireland for a year. Loo Lave Adda is a phonetic attempt at Lugh Lámhfhada, Lugh of the long hand, in origin a Celtic deity, hero and master of all the arts; he was not the son of Con. Lugh led the otherworldly Tuatha Dé Danann to victory in the fabulous Battle of Moytura, said to have occurred a few miles west of The Neale. Edna or Edana was a poet and prophetess of the Tuatha Dé Danann. The jumble of figures in the middle of the inscription are dates; AM stands for Anno Mundi, the 'year of the world' in the system based on the date of Creation, 4004 B.C., concocted by Bishop Ussher in the seventeenth century; what the other abbreviations stand for I do not know. The old idea that the village name, The Neale, is an anglicization of the Irish An Fhéile, the festival, felicity or generosity, is not favoured by place-name experts nowadays.

Estate records of The Neale say the various follies were designed by Lord Charlemont, whose sister married Sir John Browne, later to become the first Baron Kilmaine, in 1764. But Charlemont was an enthusiast for classicism (the Casino at Marino in Dublin was his pleasure house, and his main residence, Charlemont House, is now the Dublin City Gallery), so even if he is responsible for the symmetrical form of the monument, which tapers upwards stepwise to a little pedestal bearing a stone sphere (now missing), he would not have approved either the style or the substance of the garbled inscription. The first investigator to transcribe the plaque was seemingly the travel writer and actor Richard Hayward in 1941 or 1942; a unionist with nationalistic sympathies, he dismisses the monument as a whim of the irresponsible landlord class: 'a more absurd conglomeration of unrelated objects never confronted the eyes of man.' In stark contrast, the archaeologist Peter Harbison writes:

> The inscription and the whole monument should be seen not just as a piece of romantic dilettante erudition, but also as an extraordinary piece of reverence to the Celtic past by a member of the landed aristocracy in the west of Ireland.

Is it possible then that the date 1753 at the end of the inscription refers to a reestablishment of the worship of the ancient Irish gods by members of the landlord's family? What trace, what presence, might such a cult have left in the atmosphere of this ruinous and over-grown corner? Looking around me, I thought of M. R. James' *Ghost Stories of an Antiquary*; all the props of an incipient tale in his vein were here: the unfrequented ruin, the puzzling inscription, the premature dusk gathering under the trees. I did not linger, but found my way back to the hole in the wall and scrambled out into the coolly rational summer afternoon.

The above account is an accurate reflection of this curious experience, written in a B&B in Connemara five or six hours later, bulked up with some material from subsequent research. But before I looked it up in my diary my clear and unarguable memory of the episode was somewhat different. Soon after leaving the commonplace little town I became aware of the absence of traffic. The broad, shallow farmlands breathed a disquieting silence. The first person I saw on the road was an elderly man on a bicycle; I caught up with him just as we passed the monument with nine tall steps leading up to nothing. I asked him what it was, and he told me about the landlord who had had his hungry tenantry build it in the famine time. Then he went on to urge me, insistently, to visit the Gods of the Neale, the nature of which entity he could not articulate. A little further on we passed a small community hall that, he told me, was named from a young republican killed in 1921 by the Black and Tans in the Tourmakeady ambush. We went on to talk of the troubles in the North, which were at their most murderous at that time. Recognizing that I was English, he hastened to tell me that the history being taught nowadays made the present IRA think they were emulating the old IRA of the War of Independence, which they were not; I was not to think that Irish people in these parts had any sympathy for those people.

When we parted he continued westwards and I turned down the lane he had told me would lead me to the mysterious Gods. The children in the village school playground pointed me on my way; I climbed from sunlight into tree-shadow through the broken-down demesne wall with a sense of achievement, of escape from the everyday net of public ways, into the realm of the unexpected. The monument reared up before me as I parted the rampant vegetation. I took out my notebook and set myself busily to transcribe its inscription, perhaps to disperse the rather oppressive eeriness of its unfrequented and neglected setting. I could only make it out in parts and by degrees, but this much was clear: '. . . Lett us follow their stepps sick of love with FVLL confidence in Loo Lave Adda . . . the Shepherd of Ireland of his era . . .' What exactly did that mean? What did 'sick of love' mean in the eighteenth century? Are we tired of loving our old ways, or overcome by love of these new or rediscovered gods?

The antique stones had nothing to add. I dismissed as over-imaginative a twinge of anxiety, a faint premonition of nightmare, of failing to refind the hole in the demesne wall. The birdless shrubbery, the ivy weaving its nets around the fallen masonry of the old mansion, suggested politely but firmly that I should now leave, and allowed me to do so without difficulty.

On reaching the main road again I turned westwards towards Connemara, the mountainous boundary of which reared up from the plain more and more decisively as I progressed. A few miles beyond the village I saw a figure standing in the road with a bicycle; as I approached, I realized it was the man I had met earlier. He had waited for me, he said, because he wanted to be sure I would not miss the site of the Battle of Moytura. He indicated a number of huge boulders among a few trees at the further end of a low rise in a roadside field, and having pointed out my way, or put me out of my way, once again, took himself off. I strayed among the ancient stones for some time, wondering why he had so insisted on my making this detour. I knew little about the epochal battle that took place, or has been staged by ancient storytellers, here. Later I read it up in *Loch Coirib − its Shores and Islands*, by the nineteenth-century antiquarian Sir William Wilde, who had his country home nearby. Putting together local folklore and the witness of medieval manuscripts, Wilde gives a detailed account of the battle between the magical invaders, the

Tuatha Dé Danann, or People of the Goddess Danu, and the native Fir Bolg, which raged for four days, involved a hundred thousand on either side, and left its memorials in the form of the numerous cashels, cairns and standing stones to be seen in the sleepy countryside around The Neale. Lugh, son of the Dé Danann king Nuadu, was killed in the third day's fighting and is said to be buried under one of the standing stones near the village. But in the end the Fir Bolg were defeated and took refuge in the Aran Islands, where they built the great clifftop fort of Dún Aonghasa.

However, there is a grander corpus of myth concerning another Battle of Moytura, usually said to have been fought at another Moytura in Sligo but frequently – and certainly in my mind – conflated with the Battle of Moytura in Mayo. This second battle pitched the divine Tuatha Dé Danann against the Fomhóire, a grim race of sea-pirates, and its pivotal event was the confrontation between Lugh and his grandfather Balor, a giant, perhaps a thunder god in origin, who had a single lightning-flashing eye which it took four men to open. Lugh flung his spear, or a slingshot, at this baleful eye and knocked it through to the back of his head so that it looked upon Balor's own soldiers and, according to Mayo folklore, turned them into the stones I was wandering among, somewhat empty-mindedly, that day of my journey.

Why was I here? Not one of the boulders had a word

to say. The sky was darkening, and I still had a long way to go. I returned to my bike and set off again westwards.

I broke out through the rapidly diminishing hole in the wall, breathless, my heart racing. The shrieks of the children drove me back to the junction with the main road, where I saw that the old man riding away on his bike was still only a few dozen yards distant; it was as if I had spent no time at all in the demesne, or none of the time of this world. I laboured on my bicycle but I could not catch up with him, although he seemed to be pedalling at a normal easy rate; it was because the road was slippery with blood, and my long hand impeded me. Soon he was far ahead and waiting for me near the circle of stones. The hedges for miles around were full of the sound of iron on skin, iron on flesh, iron on bone. He towered among the thunderclouds forming on the mountain rim of Connemara. In the middle of his forehead is the mark I must aim at.

Where are the Nows of Yesteryear?

Now that so much time has passed, I must admit the possibility that my childhood memories of my grandmother's musical box have been polished into luminosity by nostalgia. It stood on a low occasional table in her little antique shop, overshadowed by towering wardrobes and crowding tallboys but glinting as with an internal energy. Its simple, almost naïve, mechanism fascinated me: a spring-powered contraption like the works of an old clock drove the rotation of a brass cylinder, on which were hundreds of prickles that twanged the teeth of a graduated steel comb, producing hesitant and plaintive melodies. This tender machinery was mounted on a polished wooden base and covered by a lid with glass sides, through which I could admire the tense coiled spring and dark laborious cogs, watch the hypnotically slow turning of the gleaming cylinder, and sense the tiny flexure and straining of a tooth of the dull grey comb as each note was prepared, seemed momentarily to resist being detached from silence, and then yielded with a slight reluctance, like a ripe blackberry plucked from a briar. Years later when I read H. G. Wells' description of the Time Machine, a glittering apparatus of bronze and crystal, I was carried back to the fusty old shop in the quiet North Wales town of Mold. Had I realized then that the musical box was itself a time machine I would have asked my grandmother for it, she would have kept it for me, and it would be on my desk now.

Now, philosophers of time like to illustrate the difficulties, perhaps the impossibility, of travelling back in time, by considering the case of an imaginary time traveller who kills off one of his or her grandparents at such an early age as to preclude his own birth and thus his dreadful deed. The fascination of this traditional vein of logical argument obscures an underlying fantasy, unthinkable not only in its paradoxicality but ethically, comprising as it does both murder and an esoteric form of suicide. Among our eminent contemporaries who have scratched their heads over the paradox, Professor Hugh Mellor of Cambridge has a version that targets the grandfather, while Professor Michael Lockwood of Oxford opts for the grandmother. But if I could meet my grandparents again, far from shortening their lives I would expend a little of my own in trying to salvage at least a memory of theirs. How little I know of them! What was their background? I remember my grandmother shortly before she died telling me that her grandfather once ate his dinner off the face of the clock on the Liver

Building in Liverpool. My parents dismissed this as the ramblings of old age when I reported it to them, but I take it as truth and like to think that this great-great-grandfather of mine was a city dignitary who partook of a banquet for which the clock face served as a table, before its installation marked the completion of Liverpool's temple of mercantilism. But I know nothing about my grandparents' forebears, and indeed my memories of my grandparents themselves are hardly more than textural. When I ride back in time – on the musical box perhaps – to Mold (the very name recaptures the little town as it was when my parents used to bring me there on occasional holiday visits almost a lifetime ago), I encounter on the staircase behind the shop the soft indulgent bulk of my grandmother, and glimpse my tall, rigid, grandfather, ignoring me out of shyness rather than antipathy, turning away in the doorspace of a further room. Now that I am old enough to be the grandfather of the child I then was, I can understand something of the distance he chose to occupy, but I cannot communicate this fellow feeling, for that was then, as they say, and this is now.

Now and again I used to lose myself in two paintings hung on that staircase: 'La Rixe' (the brawl) by Meissonier, Queen Victoria's favourite painter, and Millet's 'Angelus', so much admired by Salvador Dalí. Both represent instants of stasis. In the first, a pack of cards lies scattered on the floor among overturned table, chairs and wine bottles; two gamblers have leaped to confront each other and are being restrained by their companions. One of the antagonists has a dagger; a man behind him tries to twist it out of his grasp while another seizes him around the chest. (It can hardly have been my gentle grandmother who told me that the model for the man with the dagger is said to have died of his frustrated exertions in this role.) The other would-be fighter is trying to draw his sword but is obstructed by a fifth man, who holds him back with one arm and stretches out the other towards the face of the man with the dagger, hand wide open and fingers crooked, in a gesture that shouts 'No!' so loudly that time is stopped. Every detail of the scene is meticulously rendered, though one could scarcely call the result lifelike. Meissonier masters time, and here a moment is preserved as if under brown varnish, but space is beyond him. As one critic has written, 'his prodigious power of decomposition left him incapable of putting anything together again'. And in this painting the dimension of depth is all awry; figures seem to step through each other, space is crumpled and tumbled. (But perhaps all this is masterly, Einsteinian, a General Relativity of drunken rage.) The other painting, in contrast, offers contemplative stillness. The chimes of the Angelus, conducted by a flock of rooks high in the evening sky, come from a church tower on the horizon of an endless plain, to two potato-pickers. The young couple stand with bowed heads, at their feet a half-filled basket. They are statuesque figures, alone in the vast emptiness. In one of his homages to this painting Dalí transforms them into rook-haunted ruinous towers much taller than the dark cypresses (reminiscent of those on Böcklin's 'Island of the Dead') growing around their bases. Dalí's X-ray eyes also made out that Millet had painted the potato basket over the representation of a coffin in which the two peasants had brought their dead child for burial. In another interpretation of the scene Dalí diagnoses sexual tension; he depicts the moment after that of the Angelus, in which the male peasant leaps at the female as urgently as Meissonier's furious gamesters strain to stab each other. Of course as a child I was aware of none of this. For me each of the two paintings in the staircase was a banner parading through all time an ancient and incomprehensible Now.

Nowadays analytic philosophers such as the professors mentioned above are not professionally interested in the phenomenology and, even less, the poetics of time, neither as evoked by Proust's soggy cake-crumbs nor as measured by Dalí's melting watches. Both of them pay more attention to the dry argumentation of the Cambridge philosopher John McTaggart, who in 1908 published a paper on 'The Unreality of Time'. There are, says McTaggart, two ways of describing time. One of them seems to fit our experience of time's flow; it uses such terms as past, present and future, tomorrow, a long time ago, and so on, all crucially connected with the concept of the present moment, the Now. (Today's philosophers would call this version 'tensed time'.) An event may at some time be future, then be present, and finally be past. (I can say an event 'is future', as short-hand for 'will take place in the future'; the details of English tense grammar don't enter into this discussion.) But how can an event have these contradictory qualities, of being future, present and past? Because of course it has them at different times, we rush in to say! Thus it might be that in the past it was future, at present it is present, and in the future it will be past. But this will not do, responds McTaggart; it seeks to explicate past, present and future in terms of past, present and future, and so leads us up the garden path into vicious circles. Therefore tensed time does not exist. 'Nonsense!' cries Professor Mellor (and I have seen him denounce non-sense, in a seminar on metaphysics I crept into once: a fierce, compact personage, he turns his back on the source of nonsense and curls up in his chair as if shielding himself from contamination, while his errant post-graduate students quail); future, present and past are not qualities of events, they are relationships. To remark that an event is future is to say that it takes place after the making of the remark. Thus the terminology of tensed time depends on that of tenseless time, time as ordered by the relationships 'before', 'simultaneous with' and 'after', and specified by dates such as 1066 or phrases like 'just before breakfast on Tim Robinson's fifth Christmas Day'. But this apparently objective version of time runs into difficulties too, at least in the outer reaches of modern physics. Before Einstein it could be supposed that any two observers would in principle agree as to which of two events happened first; but Special Relativity says that they may not, if they are in motion relative to each other. Indeed, as Einstein's great master Hermann Minkowski said in 1908, 'Henceforth space by itself, and time by itself, are doomed to fade away into mere shadows, and only a kind of union of the two will preserve an independent reality.' Since then spacetime itself has been proved to be warped, to be expanding, probably to have a beginning and perhaps an end, to contain holes, to be stuffed with six or seven other dimensions tightly curled up like subatomic horsehair. This welter of wonders entails impenetrable complications for the theory of time, seeming to imply that the concepts of past, present and future have at the most a local and almost a person-specific degree of adequacy. Professor Lockwood's book on the subject is admirably lucid, but its title gives due warning: *The Labyrinth of Time*. I used to think I comprehended these matters, but I am not so sure of my grip on time as of now.

Now, or never, having awoken my grandparents' old house from the comfortable doze it has enjoyed in my memory for so long, is the time to record another aspect of it, before the mice of forgetfulness gnaw it all away. Behind the front ground-floor room occupied by the shop, down a few stairs, was a semi-basement – a mere coal-hole, I suppose, but it seemed spacious to me – into which coke used to be avalanched every now and then through a hatch in the rear wall of the house. I liked to stand on a wooden step by the coke-hill and look out of this hatch, my chin on a level with the cobbles of the back lane. Opposite, the parish church towered among tall trees. The shadowy space between the backs of the houses and the churchyard wall was projected into the unreal by my worm's-eye perspective on it. When, just now, I summoned up maps and photographs from the internet I found that this little region of mystery no longer exists; the back lane and the terrace houses of which my grandparents' was one have been swept away and replaced by a sloping lawn, a civic amenity offering a view of the old church from the main street. The lane mattered to me because it led to a children's playground with a few swings, a small roundabout, and a pair of parallel bars. As a devotee of Tarzan I was proud of my ability to hang by my knees from one of these bars. My head must have been close to the ground in this position, for once when my long-suffering knees relaxed their grip I came down with a thump that sent me wailing back along the lane, but did no visible damage to my skull. (I could say that I have never been the same since, but that is true of every moment of my life.) My image of myself upside-down, bat-like, in the rectangular space below the bar, like that of myself at the hatch with my chin on its sill, gives me a measure of my size at that time of my life. Our subjective experience of the flow of time, says Hugh Mellor, is no evidence that time really does flow; what we actually experience is change in ourselves, the accumulation of memories, of memories of memories. This must include memories of stages in physical growth, and of the incidents that knock such memories into our heads. My brief surrender to gravity, my tearful return down the lane, are lodged in the loops of my brainstuff, as are my grandfather quelling my sobs with the testy formula, 'Now then!' and my grandmother applying as a verbal salve to my sore head a soft dove-like repetition of 'Now, now . . .'

Now, and to end, let me open what always felt to me to be the secret heart of my grandparents' house. At floor-level in a corner of the sitting room was a cupboard full of games that must have been oldfashioned even in those days of my childhood. Sometimes I would delve into it before breakfast, when there was a faint acrid tang of dead ashes in the room, as yet unvisited by the day's routines. There were tiddlywinks and marbles, packs of cards for playing Happy Families, and shallow boxes that opened up into trays scattered with cardboard fish one could angle for with a little magnet on a string. On the floor of the cupboard, or between the leaves of big illustrated books, I used occasionally to find more valuable fish too, escaped perhaps from a long-lost pouch; they were delicately cut out from wafers of a pearly, translucent material, and must have been tokens in an antique parlour game, as I realized much later when I read in a Jane Austen novel of a young lady who after an evening visit could talk of nothing but the fish she had won and the fish she had lost. Most precious of all was a set of ivory spillikins in a narrow little box, also of ivory, with a delicately fretted lid. Each spillikin had a slender stem some five inches long, and a head representing a Chinese sage, a sickle moon, a long-tailed bird or some odd animal. Piled on a tabletop, they formed a tangle from which with the aid of a little hook one tried to extricate one spillikin at a time without causing the least trembling amongst the rest, an operation as delicate as that of capturing an elusive memory without awakening others interlinked with it that one would rather leave undisturbed. Where is this test of the subtle and steady hand now? At the bottom of a box of crumpled letters, photographs and ephemera, perhaps, forgotten in the attic of some house I have long quitted. And the moment of first finding them, in my grandparents' cupboard? All events have equal claims to a tenseless reality, says Professor Mellor; all have their address in spacetime. Among them must be the contents of everyone's Nows, whether past, present or future, remembered or forgotten, observed or unobserved. While it is not quite pleasing to hear that countless redundant trivialities are of the stuff of the universe, I like to think that the particular Nows that have been picked out by our passionate attention to them are stacked away separately, as it were in vaults, like paintings bought by a millionaire on the advice of experts. If the connoisseurship of memory is the human role in this indiscriminately memorious world, then among those treasures is certainly my grandmother's quietly challenging utterance on first emptying out the box of spillikins for me: 'Now!'

The Tower of Silence

We said goodbye at the gate.
His first step took him over the horizon.
We stood around his parting footprint.
'He must be taller than we thought,' we said.

We met him near the West Hampstead tube station: a young man we knew little of beyond the fact that he, like us, lived in a house that was awaiting demolition. He had a small bag slung over one shoulder. 'Where are you off to?' we asked. 'Kathmandu,' he replied, and strode onwards.

That evening I mentioned him to Anna, founder of the local self-help organization that had argued the Council into letting some of its stock of unoccupied housing be used temporarily by such indefinables as ourselves and the Kathmandu pilgrim. She had not known of his departure, but we were all as elusive as eels, and she was unsurprised. The next day she went to the house to see if it was suitable for others of her houseless clients. 'He's left a few old books you might be interested in,' she said to me later, 'and the house itself is worth seeing.'

Lured by the whiff of old books, I hurried round there myself. The house, Victorian, detached, three storeys and attic over a semi-basement, stood in a tangle of scrawny buddleia bushes. The back door to the basement flat gave at my push. I stepped in, and stood amazed. The ceiling of the flat's main room together with the floors and ceilings of the room above it, and of the one above that, and the one above that, had been removed. The departed resident must have started in the attic by prising up the floorboards and sawing through the joists beneath them, and so on down from floor to floor. I saw no sign of the piles of timber this operation must have produced; perhaps they had been sold to fund his travels. One wall of the great empty tower had a door in it at each level, all hanging open; another wall had four tiled fireplaces one high above another. Craning my neck I could make out some flowers, still fresh-looking, in a jamjar on the topmost mantelpiece.

After some rooting around in cupboards and cardboard boxes I found the books. They were mouldy and battered, but a nineteenth-century guide to Wales with engravings of famous views was worth salvaging. Then a ragged volume with the title *Sahara,* or perhaps *Saraha,* caught my eye. It seemed to be the work of a Buddhist sage of some such name. I dipped into the long and scholarly introduction, and flipped through the many detailed notes at the end of the book. Intrigued, I eagerly turned to the text itself, only to find that it had been ripped out. What I had in my hand was the husk, academic analysis and pedantic commentary; the precious kernel, the divine message, was gone – to Kathmandu, no doubt.

The Tower of Silence always stands in a city somewhere. No street-noise reaches its summit. With every dawn it gives itself a new horizon. The doorman is polite but remote.

One day when the Tower was in Istanbul I stepped out of it into what had been the courtyard of a Venetian caravanserai. The domes of the arcade had long fallen in. Squatting below the ragged circles of sky were women, their hands busy picking rags to bits, sorting short lengths of thread by colour. In Terre Haute, Indiana, right opposite the doorway of the Tower, were the boarded-up windows of an apartment once used by the prostitute Al Capone blamed for his gonorrhoea and sent one of his gang to murder. In Paris when I went to cross the road from the Tower's splendid porte-cochère I had to step around two weeping women locked in each other's arms. They had just come out of the Institut Curie's radiotherapy centre, having, I surmised, just received the results of tests; the younger woman had burst into tears as soon as they were free of the Institut's constraining orderliness, and the elder, her mother perhaps, was comforting her. In Dubrovnik the Tower's lobby formed part of the promenade around the city walls and faced the back of the jail. Something small was hanging on a string from the bars of a little window: a Turkish cigarette package, ten Bafras, empty, blue. A vortex of traffic separated the Tower's front steps from the blood-cemented stones of the Coliseum in Rome. There were so many people crossing the street on which the Tower stood in the City of London that some of them had to step over the little drunken Scotsman lying on his back agitating his limbs like a capsized beetle. The Lion Dance went round and round the Tower in Bangkok; the six capering monkeys, their masks lumpy coagulations of spite, harried the exhausted lion, which feebly snapped its huge jaws at them. The child who slept among the Tower's dustbins in Calcutta had dragons of pleated paper for sale; he could make one of them run up onto the back of another as if in copulation. His mother in Dublin sat against one of the Tower's plant containers all day and apparently owned nothing but a plastic cup. When the Tower returned to Istanbul there was a man living in the concrete-pillared parking space under it. The bottom half of his body had been replaced by a curved piece of rubber cut from a tyre, and he swung himself along by means of two weights in his hands. As I watched he levered himself off a step onto a lower one, bounced and fell over with a curse. Two other men lurking in the darkness further back laughed at him. And so on, world without end.

Parallax

My father had a curious habit of closing one eye and tilting his head slightly while staring into space. This behaviour could be disconcerting when it occurred during a conversation, as it appeared to be a momentary withdrawal of engagement with the matter in hand. I suppose those familiar with it dismissed it as a nervous tic, or a lapse into deep thought. But I knew what it was, because I have inherited it. He was bringing into alignment two points at different distances from the eye; for instance, if he was indoors it might have been a corner of a window pane and the tip of a twig in a bush outside. I never asked him what the practice meant to him; it was so obviously part of his interior and perhaps unconscious life that to mention it would have been intrusive and made him uncomfortable. Nor do I know whether it was elaborated in him, as it is in me, into a search for geometrical forms in whatever lies before my eyes, seen as if it were a depthless projection onto a screen. In my case I can connect it with the fascination with geometry and mathematics in general that took me to Cambridge long ago and still informs or intrudes upon my writing even on subjects remote from the exactly definable. Perhaps this elevation of a visual obsession into an intellectual discipline is self-protective. Pity the St Sebastians of geometry; right angles, triangles, parallel lines, tangential contacts, pour in upon them and pierce them. These forms are generated by points: the exact centre of a round mirror, a fly on the wall, a far-off chimney-top, the first star of evening, an evanescent crank in the profile of a cloud. Points of light or darkness, rays seen endways on, compose themselves restlessly into nameable patterns, diagrams, theorems, pictures. When the thornbush outside my window begins to fill with incompatible geometries as with gibbering monkeys, it is time to draw the curtain.

But I fear being deprived of this ocular food. Suppose my bedroom here were even more featureless than it is, a bare cell, or, more drastically, reduced to the three lines I often trace when lying in my bed: the meeting of two walls with each other, and of each with the ceiling. They run unstoppably together at a point, a singularity, signalling definitive closure and denial of exit. That point is a gun barrel of perfect fineness and absolute exactitude aiming a needle at my eye.

On certain nights, by rota, I have care of another needle. Somewhere on the far side of the globe two of the tectonic plates that make up the earth's crust and carry the continents and the oceans have been locked against one another, unable to move in response to the sluggish convection currents in the magma on which they rest. Tension has been building for decades, for centuries. Now, perhaps at this very moment, great thicknesses of rock are tearing like paper as the plates lurch onwards, accomplishing a few more feet or yards of their blind journey. The shock generates pressure waves that radiate through the interior of the earth, where they may be reflected off or pass through the inner core, a solid sphere of iron and nickel some 1500 miles across. There are shear waves too, that shake the rock from side to side like a dog with a rat; they cannot pass through liquids such as the molten rock of the outer core, so take their way through the crust and the plastic but near-solid magma of the mantle. Both types of waves also travel around the surface of the globe, causing the ground to roll like a slow-motion ocean and to shudder laterally in a way that near the epicentre of the earthquake can topple cities. These various waves interfere with one another and sound out the earth's fundamental frequencies, and are eventually attenuated by distance until only the most delicate of instruments can detect them. Our seismograph is an elaborate construction of balanced levers that translate the relative displacement of a weight and the casing from which it is suspended into the oscillations of a needle across the moving surface of a roll of smoked paper; thus an earthquake in

Chile or China can write itself into the scientific record by displacing grains of soot half a world away. Many of the observatories housing such devices are or were manned by Jesuits; our Order's intellectual traditions and its wide spread of institutions fitted it to host much of the seismographical network, humanity's dispersed eye upon its own shaky foundations.

'Existential precarity is our birthright,' is a favourite saying of the greybeard set to watch over the ever-vigilant device. From moment to moment all might end; to live is to live dangerously. Consider these grains of soot tumbled aside by the swinging pen. He bends over them with a magnifying glass. They are craggy boulders of some dark igneous rock, with black screes on their shoulders. He sneezes, they disappear. The air is hung like a Christmas tree with the microscopic globules of his infected rheum. As usual, I relieve him at midnight. Within a few days I am confined to bed in a meagre cuboid of space off the sickroom. My obsessions are feverous. Even when the darkness is absolute, ceiling and walls play their game, colluding in corners. Three go into one, and that one an exception, a singularity. It is a sink, avidly draining form out of the room, emptying emptiness. My mind goes whirling down the vortex.

Cosmologists speculate that the singularity, the point at the heart of a collapsed and burned-out star where pressures and temperature become infinite, could be the budding-point of a new universe. This unreachable other world might be unimaginably different from ours: a hell, or a paradise, or devoid of creatures to feel the difference. If universes give rise to universes eternally and ours is a bubble in the foam of an infinite multiverse, then any material order consistent with the laws of physics, however improbable, will obtain in an infinity of other universes. There are perhaps countless universes differing from ours in this particular only, that my father would not have been afflicted with his point-alignment compulsion, and therefore that I, in whom, thankfully, the line ends, would not have inherited it.

Shadows and Eclipses

In the summer of 1968 I went wandering in Provence, a left-over sun-shrunken scrap of the Roman Empire. From the village of Saint-Rémy, which once sheltered Van Gogh's anguish, I crossed the stony hills called Les Alpilles. There were 'no smoking' notices among the grotesque wind-racked pine trees, for the atmosphere was explosive, heavy with resinous exudations. Then I descended to the sun-smitten streets of Arles, where I found a museum, which I entered for the sake of shade. It had, I read in my guidebook, been founded by Mistral, the nineteenth-century poet who wrote the dying Provençal language and culture back into life. His very name – borrowed from the occasional biting north wind that comes avalanching down mountain slopes in the Rhône valley – proposed the opposite of the unmerciful sun.

The shadowy and dusty interior came close to my idea of the perfect museum. It was so crammed with exhibits that my mental records of them have strangled each other, all except that of one cryptic item: a hen's egg with a shallow indentation on one side, in the shape of a circle from which a few broad grooves radiated. The notice beside it was terse: 'Egg laid during an eclipse.' This object appealed to me as the ideal museum piece, the mysterious deposition of a culture, the condensate of intricate eclipses that occur when the moon, the earth and the sun are aligned, or nearly so. If the earth lies between the sun and the moon, the earth casts its shadow on the moon. If the moon is between the earth and the sun, the moon casts its shadow on the earth. In the first case, the face of the moon visible from the earth is fully illuminated apart from the area shaded from the sun by the earth. That is why eclipses of the moon occur at full moon. In the second case, the face of the moon visible from earth is turned away from the sun and is in shadow; hence, eclipses of the sun occur at new moon. During a new moon eclipse, to an observer situated on the part of the earth's surface overshadowed by the moon, the latter appears as a black disc moving across the face of the sun and obscuring it in full or in part. By coincidence the apparent sizes of sun and moon as seen from the earth are roughly the same, and so it is possible for the moon to hide the sun completely for a brief time. Since the moon's orbit round the earth is not quite circular but elliptical, the distance between the two varies cyclically, as does the apparent size of the moon's disc. If an eclipse of the sun occurs when the moon is at its apogee or greatest distance from the earth, and therefore its apparent size is at its minimum, it cannot totally obscure the sun, and may appear as a black disc with a rim of fire.

What would it be like to observe these phenomena from one side, say from some other planet? Light in general is invisible unless it falls on a retina, either directly from its source or by reflection from an illuminated surface; light rays passing in front of the eye do not interfere with those entering the eye. Since the space in which the sun and its planets pursue their courses is empty apart from extremely tenuous dust clouds, the sun's rays are reflected only from such surfaces as that of the moon and the earth. Astronomical shadows, therefore, are only seen by contrast with illuminated surfaces; they do not show up in empty space as dark bands or shafts as shadows do in misty air. So for the extraterrestrial observer introduced above, the shadow of the moon is only visible during a solar eclipse, when it shows up as a dark circle on the otherwise illuminated surface of the earth. Similarly, the shadow of the earth is only visible during a lunar eclipse, when it appears as a dark area on the otherwise illuminated surface of the moon. If another body such as an asteroid were to pass behind the moon, relatively to the sun, the extraterrestrial would see it as a dot, shining by reflection of sunlight, that winks out as it enters the zone from which the moon blocks off the sun's rays. This zone comprises the actual shadow of the moon, visible by contrast on the surface of the earth during eclipses, plus its potential shadow made up of all the points at which its shadow would be visible if there were a surface there for it to inscribe itself on.

As a potentially reflective object I cannot enter the moon's zone of potential shadow without actualizing part of it as shadow on my own surface. This fact of physics precludes me from seeing my unshadowed self by the absent light of a lunar eclipse. Full moon and new moon are such by virtue of the collapse into a line of the triangle formed by earth, sun and moon; eclipses are the mark of the most complete and perfect of such compressions of space. If it were possible to interfere with geometry, I could hold open such a triangle and slip through it into the zone of potentiality, either that of the earth or that of the moon. In these impossible circumstances I, as a sun-maddened, or let me say a sun-warmed creature, would see my own shadow from the inside, as it were. Suppose I were on the nocturnal side of the earth during a solar eclipse, looking down a hole passing through the centre of the earth to what would be, if it were not for the interruption of the sun's rays by the moon, its daylight side; then I, no, I mean to say, if I were on the diurnal side of the earth and looking through it by means of such a hole as described, during a lunar eclipse, I would see on the shadowed moon the image of the hole, illuminated, and within that frame my own shadow. To be absolutely accurate and comprehensive about this thought-experiment, I should admit that it would require telescopic eyes, for my shadow and the image of the illuminated window around it would occupy an almost infinitesimally small portion of the distant moon's dark face. Nevertheless, the principle stands, I believe.

The geometry of the triangle mentioned above calls for elucidation. In the case of an impending lunar eclipse the earth marks the vertex of the triangle opposite its longest side, which is under varying tension as the earth moves into perfect alignment with the sun and the moon, passes through this position and proceeds into space on the other side of the triangle's longest side, or since all these positions are relative to each other perhaps it would be clearer to say that as the moon pursues its orbit around the earth and the earth its orbit around the sun, the latter approaches, attains to and abandons a position on an extension of the earth/moon side of the celestial triangle. Were it not for the impermeability of the vacuum to sound, this growth and release of tension might be heard as a musical note like that of a harp string, and indeed I believe this to be the origin of the Pythagorean theory of celestial harmony. I should have written, above, that the extension of the earth/moon line sweeps through space and approaches, etc., the sun, instead of the other way round. The outcome is the same, of course: the emission of an inaudible note in the Harmony of the Spheres. To one who has ears for such sublimities I recommend a study of the interactions of the shadows actual and potential described above and the sides and vertices of the imaginary but musical celestial triangle. But how can I convey the subtleties of this tenuous matter? Am I stable enough to pick my way without tripping through the tangles of, triangles of, sound unheard and shadow unseen?

The half-moon is of course exempt from eclipse. At six o'clock of an equinoctial evening it perches on the chimneypot of the old schoolteacher's cottage with its flat side exactly vertical, single silver breast of the night, a cup spilling half the stars there are conversely does the warp and weft of sublunary and transundance Sunwise transident spidersweb cohere sufficiently to keep me aloft for long enough to let me observe the inwork of creation the invisible ink of creation from above or from outside its all-inclusive tenuities or am I at risk of falling falling falling falling Icarus into a sea of error and con-tradiction and inexactitudes and approximents to truth but a miss is as bad as a mile where all that counts is all that counts is all that counts perhaps to start agon again an agon with the simplest condsiderialities such as the diffention of an ecl As this: Eclipses occur when the moon, the earth and the sun are aligned, or nearly so if the earth lies between the sun and the moon, the earth casts its shadow on the moon if the moon is between the earth and the sun the moon casts its shadow on the earth in the first case the face of the moon visible from the earth is fully illuminated apart from the area shaded from the sun by the earth. I suspect error in all this, or terror. Slivered in the moon's eclipse was my birth triangle, a a a a beginning of lifelong hesitation too slow a a a a beginning of lifelong hesitation too slow for heaven when the sun shines on its own shadow from inside, so much so that, when M and I holidayed in Provence many years later, I insisted we visit the museum of the time-lain egg. But I found the place much changed. The corridors had been cleared of what the act of clearance itself would have defined as clutter. Despite curtains drawn over the windows, the air was hot and stagnant. The attendants – three or four young women – seemed to be not so much wearing as crammed into Provençal costumes, stifling complications of aprons, skirts, petticoats, scarves and bonnets. One of them, evidently a new recruit, was being trained to pace the galleries; she was already bored and frustrated, on the verge of hysterics. As blindly angry as a wasp against glass, she marched the length of a central aisle, turned with a stamp of a foot and marched back again, her expression almost audibly crying, 'That was a stupid waste of effort.' To avoid a situation that looked as if it might open like a carnivorous flower into a screaming row, we took to the minor aisles and bent our attention to the highly polished vitrines. Their contents were spaciously laid out, with every item clearly and informatively labelled. Identification, classification, order reigned. Despite the heat

I felt a chill wind descending from the heights of rationality. But of the egg of the eclipse there was no sign. If it had hatched in the meantime surely a stuffed cockatrice would have been on show. But we knew without consulting the attendants or whatever senior curator might have been disinterred from some distant office that the egg had been purged, as being too bizarrely folkloric. Of course nobody in authority there could have known that for twenty years it had eclipsed the whole of Provence in the mind of a wanderer.

Orient Express

In the early sixties M and I used to travel from Istanbul, where we were both teaching at institutions that later became the University of the Bosphorus, to Vienna or Venice for holidays, on trains that crawled from stop to stop across the intervening communist countries as if they were dragging behind them the tattered glories of the pre-War Orient Express. M had an enviable ability to sleep out endless hours in those scruffy compartments stuffed with people and baggage; I would stand in the narrow corridors and watch darkness or dawn, and occasionally slip off to the toilet with a little methylated-spirits heater to brew up illicit mugs of tea. Borders were occasions of long delays, tramping of boots and slamming of doors as police worked their way along the train checking our documentation and customs officers groped in our over-filled suitcases. One episode stands out in my memories of those anxious crossings. I think we must have been on our way to Vienna. We had obtained the necessary visas from the Bulgarian and Yugoslavian embassies in Istanbul, but as the train approached the Bulgarian border we realized that we had left the Bulgarian visas at home. Some miles beyond the little town of Edirne the train stopped in empty and unmemorable countryside. The crash of boots and authoritative demands inexorably approached from the head of the train, and the door of our compartment was wrenched open. We tried to explain our plight to the reassuringly young-looking Bulgarian border policeman, who had little English, was evidently at a loss as to what to do about us, soon seemed to give up on the situation and went back up the train. We relaxed, tentatively. A long stillness ensued. Then we heard more boots, and an altercation in a compartment ahead of ours, and after some slamming of doors the train began to move. A young couple – they could have been about our age – came into view on the platform, their mouths hanging open, eyes round with surprise, palms turned forward in appeal, as they wailed, 'Mais nous avons les

visas!' It took me a few moments to realize that they had been thrown off the train in ¶
Quick-witted M realized instantly that they must have been ejected in mistake for us. She ¶
mistake for us. By then, though we were accelerating away, away, and pounding onwards ¶
leaped at the communication cord and gave it a tug that brought the train to a groaning ¶
towards our next confrontation, at the Bulgarian-Yugoslavian frontier. There, the ¶

halt, from which, jerkily, as if under protest, it backed
slowly to the platform. The French ¶

Bulgarian border police, after some puzzling, decided
that as their colleagues had for ¶

couple reappeared, lugging their suitcases past our
window. Then we heard the boots ¶

some reason let us into the country without visas it
would be for the best to let us out, and ¶

coming our way, and unsmiling functionaries ushered
us off the train, which soon began ¶

so, our Yugoslavian documentation being in order, on
we rolled. Over the years this odd ¶

to move forward again. The French couple were
leaning out of their carriage window, all ¶

incident shaped itself into an anecdote, which I used as
our contribution to round-the- ¶

smiles, blowing kisses to us. In another minute we
were standing alone on the platform, ¶

table conversation. I would speculate that there is to
this day a little French restaurant on ¶

on which a few thistles nodded in the wind, and some
border police were beckoning us ¶

that desolate railway platform. When one day M said
'That was the most shameful thing ¶

into a little office block. I sometimes wonder what if
any consequences did M's ¶

we ever did!' I was surprised. It had not occurred to
me that we might have done ¶

unconsidered and instinctual action have on our
subsequent lives. The immediate ¶
something about the situation; the inertia of things,
specifically the momentum of the ¶
problem, of soothing the ruffled nerves of officialdom,
was soon overcome. M found a ¶
departing train, seemed to me to have swept us out of
the zone of possible influence on ¶
Turkish banknote in her purse, and as if by negligence
left it on the desk of the most ¶
the event. But perhaps that was not so. I am, at least in
theory, a consequentialist in ¶
senior-looking of the men who crowded in to have a
look at us. Then we were pushed out ¶
ethics; to judge the rights and wrongs of an action, all
its consequences should be taken ¶
into the wind again to await the next train back to
Istanbul. So we arrived back home not ¶
into account. The weakness of the theory lies in the
impossibility of evaluating an ever- ¶
much more than twelve hours after having left it – a
short time, but long enough for one of ¶
widening circle of effects, of which even the most
delicate and remote might tip some ¶
our bohemian friends, Çem the painter, to have
installed himself in our apartment where ¶
unstable situation into cataclysm. What would the
consequences have been if we had ¶

he was entertaining a sumptuous lady with eyes like
lotus ponds. This was annoying, ¶

acted promptly? For the French couple, a reinsertion
into their planned future after an ¶

especially as we had lent him our key because, or so we
had understood, he had been ¶

alarming quarter of an hour's digression, and who
knows what accidents, happy or ¶

locked out of his studio flat by his wife, who had then
disappeared with their child, and ¶

unhappy, that future might have brought them? As it is,
their situation on the railway ¶

for whom Çem was supposed to be engaged in a
desperate search throughout the teeming ¶

platform was probably sorted out soon enough for
them to catch the next train onwards; ¶

city. Further, he had let our baby tortoise, Fred Brick,
out of his vivarium, and he was ¶

they would have had an enigmatic adventure to tell
their friends about, but a few weeks ¶

nowhere to be found. M went off to bed in a rage, and
I coldly showed our guests out, ¶

later they would feel that nothing consequential had
come of it. As for us, we might have ¶

retrieving M's slippers which Çem's ladyfriend had
appropriated. I suppose a minor ¶

abandoned our plans to visit Vienna, and so not have
met the Venus of Willendorf, the ¶

consequence of M's act is that I am writing about Fred
Brick now. (The name was my ¶

tubby three-inch-long prehistoric goddess in the great
museum there, or Karl, the failed ¶

initial misreading of that on one of London's most
grandiose monuments, Frederick Duke ¶

ballet dancer on the lookout for a rich man to give him
'something a little lovely in this ¶

of York's pillar in the Mall, on my first bedazzled visit
to the city.) Inch-long Fred, head ¶

life', or Herr Rauchinger whose wife was tortured into
madness by the Gestapo and who ¶

high, limbs labouring, was capable of a surprising turn
of speed and had to be prevented ¶

spent years in a Soviet internment camp (which he said
was a better option than a week in ¶

from marching off into the irretrievable. But the death
by starvation of a tortoise is not ¶

a German concentration camp), or the Wiener Schule
artist who painted nothing but ¶

going to derail the universe. And nothing and
everything was to be expected of Çem, as ¶

bunches of asparagus – all those strange personages
whose existence somehow persuaded ¶

we should have known by then. His studio door bore
the legend, *Ici commence l'Au Delà*, ¶

us to return to the city on the conclusion of our
contracts in Turkey, and to live there for ¶

and this 'Beyond' was stuffed with relics of his
Ottoman ancestry, which one by one ¶
three years, with no doubt the broadest, but diffuse
and ungraspable, implications for the ¶
went off to the pawnshop; I remember all too vividly a
large and lifelike, or deathlike, ¶
rest of our lives. The science of complexity tells us that
in certain situations far from ¶
drawing of an impaled man wearing an elaborate
turban, and a nineteenth-century oil ¶
equilibrium an infinitesimal change in the initial
configuration of a system can cause ¶
painting of a naked beauty being paraded before a
reclining pasha. But Çem was a ¶
utterly unpredictable divergences in the course of its
evolution. The psychic system of an ¶
professional charmer, and we made it up with him
before leaving for our belated holiday ¶
artist who has yet to find self-expression is very far
from equilibrium, helplessly open to ¶
in Vienna a few weeks afterwards. Did the delay make
any difference to the total effect ¶
suggestion. In Vienna I could for the first time devote
myself entirely to painting, but the ¶
of that intriguing Cold War city on us? We cannot tell;
we cannot live two lives and ¶
city weighed upon me. Most of its people had turned
their backs on a fissured and ¶

compare them. However that may be, our experience
of Vienna must have been positive, ¶
compromised past – Herr Rauchinger was not one of
them; he loved to tell us where the ¶
for when we left Istanbul for good a year later, and
after a period of rootless wandering in ¶
bones were buried – and this ambient poison harried
my painting into nightmare. It was ¶
the Austrian Tyrol and Trentino that almost led M into
a nervous breakdown, we returned ¶
only shortly before leaving it for London that my
skeletonized birds falling through a ¶
to Vienna, and lived there for three years as I made the
first steps in my career as a ¶
vacuum suddenly and unexpectedly metamorphosed
into buoyant and celebratory ¶
painter. And such is the compartmentalised nature of
our past that we then moved on, ¶
Winged Victories. Art, thenceforth, put the
beginnings of a platform under my ¶
bringing with us very little in the way of connections
with that period of our lives, at least ¶
instabilities. It could have been a shaft of sunlight
resting on some baroque façade of Old ¶
not knowingly. Whatever we buried in Vienna remains
unexhumed by this present ¶
Vienna released me from darkness. ¶
exercise of voluntary memory. ¶

Two Cries, Two Cliffs

Eurydice in Hades

Last Wednesday, which is only a week ago, M and I strolled out from our flat in West Hampstead to a little second-hand bookshop half a mile away on Cricklewood Lane. Having looked along a short shelf, she picked out one book, then sat down and explored no further. On the way home she stopped on the steep part of Messina Avenue and told me she was exhausted. I said that, in view of the life-shaping decisions we had been living with for some months, this was no wonder; and I took her hand. We went on homewards, at a relaxed pace and in harmonious mood.

Arrived, I went into the kitchen, made us tea, and brought it into the living room. When I placed M's cup before her, with some trivial remark, her response was obscure. She mouthed something, with a faint smile; I asked her how she felt, and could make nothing of her answer. I spoke again; she was obviously trying to articulate a reply but failing to bring to mind the words she needed. Her gaze was wandering, vague. I knelt before her and hugged her, pleaded with her to tell me what was wrong. There was a froth of saliva on her lips. Language had left her, like leaves blown off a tree.

At that moment the doorbell rang. It was Anna, M's lifelong friend; she had two pots of hyacinths in her hands, one of which, it seemed, was for us. I cut short her explanations and brought her into the living room. M was lying obliquely in her chair, head flung back, mouth and eyes gaping. Suddenly she arched her back and howled. I had never heard so terrifying a sound. It was not a shriek of human pain but a long low-pitched animal roar, very loud. I seemed to see that noise as a burst of flame racing through her brain. I tried to ring our doctor's surgery, but could not get through. Anna was already calling the emergency services on her mobile phone; when they answered she handed the phone over to me. I tried to follow the instructions a responder gave me, but it was impossible to hold M's head as instructed and handle the phone at the same time; nor could we get M off her chair and spread her out on the floor, for by now she was convulsing, great shudders running down her arms and upper body. As she quietened I did not know if my lifelong love was alive or dead. Then she partially focused her eyes on me; it was like a crack opening in a wall. But the empty speech-bubbles still clustered on her lips.

Then through the window we glimpsed figures in high-visibility vests running down the street from where an ambulance was parked. Anna let them in, and one of them, a young woman, announced that she was now in charge of the scene of the incident, so I relinquished the phone and, while the medics spread M out on a stretcher, hurried around collecting an assortment of items that might be wanted. In no time at all we tumbled into the ambulance, and while it lurched and howled down the street the leader struggled to find a vein in M's arm and attach her to a plastic bag full of some elixir of life suspended above her.

My memories of the following days are confused. We arrived at the hospital in the early evening; Anna went home to her family obligations when it became clear that no immediate developments were likely, and over the next twelve hours we – a little procession: M somnolent on a trolley, a porter, a nurse, myself – trundled from cubicle to cubicle repeatedly, as in some complex board game, as new arrivals in worse shape than we were had to be accommodated. I dozed on chairs, wandered down silent but watchful corridors, found an urn dispensing hot water for tea, was given a small bag of crisps by a stranger. At five in the morning a bed was located for M, and I slept intermittently beside it, and when M became more lucid I tried to tell her what had happened. When she was fed, I scrounged a few bites off her plate. But I was not allowed to spend a second night in the ward, and so took myself home, and slept deeply.

Four mornings after the seizure, on my arrival in the

ward, I found M sleeping peacefully. I sat and watched over her. When she stirred I greeted her with a gentle hullo and waved to her through the liana-like medical paraphernalia hanging between us. She awoke rejuvenated, sprang out of bed with a glad cry and a flood of words; she seemed to me to be washed in silver light. She had been thinking: never again, she said, would she tell a troubled young friend of ours to pull himself together; never again would she tell me to straighten my shoulders. She overflowed with love, and I was an Orpheus come to lead her out of the underworld, and who would not look back. But this was a euphoria induced by the steroids she was taking; since that blissful reunion, looking back has shown us that we have stumbled frightfully close to the brinks of cliffs.

Creatures of air and earth

In writing about cliffs, not a centimetre of exaggeration is necessary or even permissible; all cliffs worth writing about are frightful. The cliff on the brink of which the following misadventure took place is part of the magnificent range of sheer precipices forming the Atlantic coastline of the island of Árainn. They rise to nearly three hundred feet in places but at the point in question are only about a hundred feet high. But that was enough to shake me like a rat in the jaws of a terrier.

Clay is a rarity in Aran; the glaciers of the last Ice Age scraped the rocks clean of it. But in some places along the rim of the cliffs there are crevices full of clay, consolidated, smoothed and bevelled off by millennia of rain and spray. One of these, a cleft some three feet wide, is tempting; one could slide down the bulge of it into a little rock-floored alcove of the cliff face, from which one would surely have a fine lateral view of waves crashing against huge blocks of stone fallen from the cliff faces of a great embayment. One day I did this.

My friends had wandered farther along the island, leaving me craning to see the fulmars (magnificent in flight but almost helpless on land) swerving through the air to land on the ledges of the cliff, tucking their degenerate little legs under them and resting on their bellies. I eased myself down the slope of clay onto the flat rock sill of the alcove, and peered round a projection of the cliff face at the fulmars, some of which were just a few feet from me; one of them, a male surprised in the act of coupling, launched himself into thunderous emptiness directly from his mate's back. I was intruding into a space not mine.

I turned to scramble back up to the cliff top. The sleek clay slope confronted me, offering no handhold. The rock on either side of it was equally smooth and unhelpful. I am no climber; in all my years of sticking my head out from the cliffs' rims to sketch the ledges and crevasses so familiar to the bird-hunters of Aran's bygone centuries I had never before ventured even so small a step in their ways. There was some sparse vegetation above the clay, just out of my reach; but it seemed to me that if I stood back far enough to take a leap and grab onto it, I would be horribly near the dizzy outer edge of the rock slab I was standing on. It would be shameful to have to shout to my friends; in any case if they had missed me they would have assumed I had wandered off botanizing and dreaming in the stony little fields of the interior. It was unlikely that anyone else, tourist or islander, would come by this remote tract of the coast-line until my disappearance had been noted and a search mounted. A touch of panic settled upon me like a little bird on my shoulder.

But here in the right-hand edge of the clay was a round hole, just above my head. Rabbits choose to live, love and breed on the brinks of these awesome heights if outcrops of clay offer the possibility of burrowing, unlike the armour of rock covering most of the land. I thrust my fist into the hole and crooked my wrist; I had a grip, and could pull myself up a bit, enough to let me grasp a rocky protrusion and drag myself back into a world of solidity and safety. I lay and breathed for a min-ute or two, then strolled on as if nothing untoward had occurred. I did not tell my companions what had hap-pened, nor did I tell M about it on my return, nor have I written or spoken of my debt to a rabbit until this moment of writing.

The Iron Bar

The cliffs of Inishbofin, off Connemara, are very different from the orderly cliffs of Aran, carved by the ocean
out of massive horizontal layers of limestone, for here
the strata have been thrown about by multimillennial
tectonic forces, and now outcrop at every angle. Along
the uninhabited south-east coast sparsely grassed slopes
plunge at forty-five degrees or more into the sea, pro-
viding some acres of crag-riven grazing for sheep and
goats. At intervals along this coast, strata of some softer
rock slicing vertically through the rest have been worn
away by the sea to form narrow cliff-sided creeks. These
are fearsome places, with walls of blackened rock up to
eighty feet high, I would guess, at their inner ends, where
the inrushing breakers work and work at enlarging them,
excavating sea-caves that will ultimately collapse, adding
loads of rock to the litter of boulders fretting away at
the floors of the creeks. The steep slopes, often slippery
with spray, around the heads of these ravines are worn
into little terraces by the passage of sheep and have to be
negotiated with care. My lapse of care was momentary,
but took me terrifyingly close to a deadly edge.

In the old days (which outcrop like rocks in the present
times of such islands) timbers from wrecks or from car-
goes abandoned in storms were a boon for the islanders,
and the creeks were natural collectors of such jetsam.

Just above the head of one of these creeks, planted as if to mark its ancient and obsolete economic standing, is an iron bar, hammered into a crack in the rock, from which the bold lads of the island used to shin down on a rope when the tide was out. This rod, red with rust for many decades, stands like a beacon of human enterprise against the savage black rocks and white foam below it; I determined to photograph it against the dark gulf. This was not easy, the terrain around the opening of the gulf being too steep to stand on securely while manoeuvring for a legible perspective. I had disburdened myself of my shoulder bag, stuffed with maps, notebook, collecting-jar, bottle of orange juice, sandwiches etc., and it lay on the slope a few yards away from me. Out of the corner of my eye I saw it lean over as if with deliberation and begin to roll lazily towards the cliff edge. Without thought I leaped down the slope to retrieve it, and then lay pinned to the turf by gravity and breathless with the realization of how near I had come to the brink. In my mind an image of myself turning in the air, dwindling, dwindling, dwindling, and then plummeting into the white surge below, was insistent for some days after that, and for many a night.

The Mother

One night a few years ago the telephone rang, and a woman's voice unleashed a flood of Connemara Irish mixed with some English. It took me some time to realize that I was being threatened with the High Court and 'the finest lawyers in Ireland', and longer for me to calm her enough to work out what was causing her evident distress. A book I had collaborated on, *Connemara and Elsewhere,* was soon to be published, and she feared that in it I might have mentioned the trial of her son on a charge of rape and murder, which I had written of in an earlier book, *Connemara: A Little Gaelic Kingdom.* The setting of this grim event was a seldom-visited bay I had explored in the course of my researches. There I had come across a little memorial like a shrine built of a few rough stones and decorated with some pathetic trinkets and reminders of the dead girl, who had been found apparently drowned in this remote spot. One of these was especially disturbing: a small plastic figurine of a kneeling girl whose short skirt did not cover her knees and who might have been pleading for her life. My account of this crime and subsequent trial had kept carefully within the bounds set by contemporary newspaper reports. I summarize:

One Saturday night some years ago three local girls queuing for a disco had some trouble with a lad they knew. He eventually took himself off. One of the girls, it turned out, was too young to be admitted to the disco, and wandered off by herself. The next day her corpse was found a mile or so away among seaweed washed into the bay. The lad was arrested on a charge of rape and murder, which he denied. He had been seen around the village both before and after an alarm had been raised over the missing girl – and had changed his sweater between times. His mother was held too, and refused to answer questions about the lad's movements that night; in fact she just kept singing an Irish song. The lad was found guilty and went to jail.

Now this folkloric character, the mother whose loyalty to her son was proof against all evidence or settled fact, was materialized in the form of a distraught voice on the telephone. I explained to her that the forthcoming book was a photographic study and made no reference to her family tragedy. But why, she wanted to know, had I written about it in that other book? It couldn't have been a nice person like me who did so; it must have been those people in Dublin, publishers and so on, who put it in, for my book wasn't that sort of book at all; it was about holy wells and old history. I tried to explain the importance of including the dark as well as the light in my portrait of the area – and meanwhile I was puzzling over her suddenly fond tone and her attempt to exculpate me. Then it came back to me: many years before the event that must have divided her life into before and after, I had stayed in her house for a few days while mapping the vicinity. Later I looked up my diary entry for those days, and found what might serve as a background note on the affair:

She's from a family once well known for illicit poitin-making, and she visits them every Sunday, rowing herself out to their island. She's a cheerful odd little woman, only 38 she says, with seven children, and a language student girl lodging. Her husband is sombre, moving around slowly with his cap on all the time. The kids I enjoyed, even their noisy TV and radio on simultaneously, and them all in a heap in front of the little turf fire.

After this belated recognition scene our discourse became fragmented. While expressing deep sympathy for her I tried to defend my writing ethic; how could I not have told the story behind that little memorial, having dealt similarly with every other feature of that shoreline? But she was unshakeable. Suddenly her voice rose to a howl: 'But I'm his mother! I'm his *mother*!' And to that elemental plaint I could answer nothing.

Backwards and Digressive

1. Building Houses

Building a house for the mind and, as soon as it is built, walking out of it – that has been the pattern of my career. Cambridge, Istanbul, Vienna, London, the Aran Islands, Connemara, and now London again. Each of these location-names approximately covers a style too, and the abrupt transitions between these styles are my subject here. Roundstone Bay, beloved but wayward old neighbour, suggested it. Early in 2014 the fortnightly alignment of the sun, earth and moon gave us the usual high spring tides, and the moon's orbit happening to bring it to its nearest approach to the earth at the same time added heft to them. Coincidentally a succession of deep troughs of low pressure lifted the surface of the sea, brought storms that drove more than usual of the Atlantic Ocean into the bay, and added torrential rain to this compilation of astronomical and meteorological extremes. One effect (minor compared to many other peoples' watery woes) of this joint attack of perigee and syzygy and anticyclone was to flood our studio with six or more inches of brine.

We were away in London, and by the time we had returned most of the water had seeped out through the floor (for this is a rickety building that leans on an ancient seawall) or had been bailed out and mopped up by a devoted neighbour; nevertheless a long, chilly and dank task faced us, of emptying bottom drawers of filing cabinets, peeling apart clumped documents, and festooning the place with maps hung out like washing. As we worked our way through the seaweed-smelling rooms of the studio, we both were aware of, but perhaps hesitated to articulate, the fact that the sea had probably found its way into a tall cupboard yet to be investigated, in which were stored my paintings – works that had followed us from Vienna to London to the Aran Islands to Connemara and had hardly been seen for decades. Eventually M insisted we look into it, and I prised open its warped door. One by one we manhandled out and unwrapped the paintings. Some had dim watermarks six inches wide along their lower edges; others had blotchy areas of damp; one was at first glance fit only to be scrapped. But many had survived unscathed, and after an initial aghast inspection it was as if the damage done to others could be lifted aside visually, leaving their intentions and achievements clear for scrutiny.

But what were they, these revenants from the 1960s and '70s? How did they relate to each other, and to work done since in such different media as maps and books? It was at this juncture that M suggested we arrange a series of pop-up exhibitions, more for our own information and assessments than for others', but nevertheless welcoming reactions from friends and visitors. There have been four of these brief, unadvertised and casually hung micro-shows so far; the first was a miscellany of works from all the above-mentioned periods, and it looked ragged and amateurish. The others concentrated on groups of related works from one period, and the present essay is a response to them. They betray the usual ambitions concerning public exposure, acceptance, praise, fame – but this essay does not pretend to evaluate the works either aesthetically or monetarily.

Is that true? Even the rudimentary curatorial effort we expended on them brought to light unsuspected affiliations and forgotten themes, and the works so linked became one, to some extent, and borrowed significance from each other. The further we unravelled this network of affinities the less ready we were to say of any piece, 'Not good enough. Away with it!' And the effect of this genealogical research (first in the pop-up shows, now in this writing) is to knit certain groups of works into meta-works to which all their components are essential. The risk in such a procedure is of exhibiting its elements in their comparative poverty of individual significance, and so drawing attention to weakness of execution or naivety of conception. Thus values and self-evaluation creep in at the cracks and joints of this present venture as the sea crept into our studio and started the whole thing off. Therefore I will stand up for my works and meta-works, while acknowledging their failings if and where I can bring myself to do so.

I begin with the most recent works and trace their genealogy backwards in time.

2. Maps and Marginalia

Apart from my maps, I produced few visual artworks during our time in Roundstone as I was concentrated on the literary works, of which I make brief mention here since in relation to my subject matter, the visual, they functioned as hoards of potential quotations, and otherwise carried on a parallel evolution. They are: *Tales and Imaginings* (2002); two collections of essays: *Setting Foot on the Shores of Connemara* (1996) and *My Time in Space* (2001); the two volumes of *Stones of Aran* (1986, 1995), and the three volumes of *Connemara* (2006, 2008, 2011).

A group of works on paper, rather derisively called *Doodleworks*, are the most recent creations. In 2005 I was invited to contribute a work to an exhibition of 'large drawings', curated by Jim Savage. I had never made any really large drawings, but I remembered a promise I'd made to myself, to investigate certain very small drawings of mine: the doodles that I produce without thought in the left-hand margins of my pages whenever I'm writing by hand. I ferretted through the scribbled notes and manuscripts of many of the books listed above, photocopied a selection of pages bearing the more luxuriant specimens of these flowers of an idling mind, and had them blown up and printed on rolls of paper about 2'6" across and 4' to 7' long, which we hung up like Chinese scrolls. In most cases bits of the text – the beginnings of each line – had been caught up (accidentally at first) by the process of enlargement; thus on the right hand of each scroll one had a column of broken phrases which, even if incomprehensible, was evidently the wreckage of some conscious process of thought, while on the left was a tangle of lines and dots, hatchings and crosshatchings, abortive Book-of-Kells fauna and invasive plant-life, equally evidently produced quite unconsciously. And the challenge of these twin texts or textures is to spot apparent interactions of left-hand wanderings and right-hand focus on the matter in hand or, better, in two hands. Whether the bannerlike hangings we made from these confrontations of thought and unthought quite attain to the status of works of art I am not sure, but perhaps they amount to a crude anatomical exhibition of the sinews of writing.

Another work of this period also was evoked by an invitation, this time from Simon Cutts of Ballybeg Press, who in connection with Cork's year as European City of Culture, 2005, was curating an exhibition of works on or incorporating vinyl (and it appears that many artists have used vinyl in ways other than as a ground of imagery). He proposed that we get my map of Aran blown up to make a large wall hanging; that did not inspire me, but the idea of a floor map that people could walk on grew out of it. The result was a 22-foot-long map of the three islands, at a scale that invites one to step from island to island like a giant of the Fir Bolg, the islands' mythical inhabitants in larger times. This floor map was glued down in a rough old school court-yard, and was accompanied by a notice embodying a discreet challenge to the public:

> The original Aran map was printed in an edition of several thousands, and when one copy was worn out another could be obtained. But the present vinyl edition is unique, and what will become of it remains to be seen. You are invited to walk on it, to dance on it, to write on it, to treat it as you see fit.

As it turned out, the map was treated with respect. After a month of hard wear and weather it came back to us rather creased and crumpled, with a few skateboard marks and some rather touchingly romantic graffiti. In

2010 it was exhibited again in the pillared library of the Royal Geographical Society's grand London premises, in connection with Hans Ulrich Obrist's Serpentine Gallery Map Marathon. This time we gave it a title, 'The Distressed Map of Aran', and it accumulated another layer of minor damage. We hope that it will continue for a long time to make occasional appearances on the same terms. There is perhaps an element of magical thinking in this project, that the actual islands might be spared whatever happens to the map – for the stones of Aran are more heartbreaking in their fragility than any sheet of vinyl. As a materialist I should suggest at least the beginnings of an idea as to how that magic might work, and the best I can offer would be that the experience of treading on the map could awaken a thoughtfulness about the islands, which might filter back to the islands by the devious ways of art and influence those who hold Aran's future in their practical hands, especially the islanders themselves.

The 'Distressed Map' hales me back to the making of my first map of Aran, and further back to various floor-based or ground-based artworks, realized and unrealized, dating from our last two years in London, before our removal to Aran. The first of these works, dating from 1969, was a large installation called 'Four-Colour Theorem'. This title reflected my interest in the famous hypothesis stating that four colours are enough to colour any map, however complicated, in such a way that no two adjacent 'countries' are of the same colour. An interminable and contentious computer proof of this apparently simple but fiendishly elusive statement had recently been advanced, and by chance I was at that time in touch with the rebel mathematician George Spencer-Brown, who dismissed the computer proof and claimed to be working on a radically original approach to the problem using his own weird theories of imaginary truth-values. However, my art project had no properly mathematical relationship, straight or deviant, with the deep puzzle to which its title makes a bow. My 'Four-Colour Theorem' consisted of fifty or sixty pieces of hardboard two to four feet across, each of one of four shapes and painted in one of four colours, laid out on a lawn in a walled garden of Kenwood House in Hampstead. The four shapes, constructed from straight lines and arcs of circles, were ones I had been using in large abstract paintings (to be described when I get back that far in time). Certain choice geometrical relationships between them ensured that the pieces could be laid edge to edge or corner to edge or corner to corner in an indefinite range of conformations. As with the 'Distressed Map' the public was invited to play its part, in this case by arranging and rearranging them like features of a geometrical garden. Over a wet Bank Holiday weekend, play got out of hand and my pristine and visionary world of arcs and lines was reduced to a muddy mess. (The challenge to the public of the 'Distressed Map of the Aran Islands' must have grown out of this sore lesson.)

A year later, in the Camden Art Centre, I showed an indoor version of this participatory work; it was called 'Moonfield' and was inspired by the almost incomprehensible black and white TV images of that first human step taken on the moon, which instantly changed its landscape more than millions of years had done. This time the flat shapes were presented in a large blacked-out gallery with its floor painted black. The shapes were black on one side and white on the other, and initially they lay black side up and were invisible; then as people discovered them underfoot and turned them over, a pallid moonscape came into existence. This was my last public work, before shrinking myself out of the London art world through ever smaller and more private works, as will be described below, and taking myself off to a little house from which, night after night, I could see the dim world of Aran's bare rock sheets.

3. Two Installations

I have made two attempts at forging a meta-work out of at-first-glance hopelessly disparate elements. One, *The View from the Horizon*, in the Irish Museum of Modern

Art in 1996, was a contribution to *Event Horizon,* an exhibition of European art curated by Michael Tarantino. The other, entitled *The Decision,* was shown in the Dublin City Gallery (the Hugh Lane) in 2011 as the final exhibition in an annual series, *The Golden Bough,* curated by Michael Dempsey. Each of these installations centred on a construction consisting of a yard-long white wooden rod about a third of an inch thick, suspended vertically in mid-air by twenty to thirty silk threads of various colours attached by tacks to scattered points of the high ceiling. These threads converged on and were glued into a little hole in the centre of the top end of the rod. In their upper reaches they all looked dark grey, but just above the top of the rod their colours seemed to merge into a faint iridescent blur; it was as if they were gathered together, blended and swallowed, to become the white of the rod. In the Hugh Lane show this construction represented for me the making of a decision out of a multitude of vague and incommensurate factors; hence the title of the show. (The decision I had in mind was the life-defining one that took us from London to the Aran Islands.) In the IMMA show this construction was called 'To the Centre', and I thought of it as a stride taken towards the centre of the earth.

In each of these installations two accumulations of rods lay on the floor beneath the suspended rod. The larger collection comprised twenty or so rods varying in diameter from a quarter of an inch to an inch, and in length from about three to nine feet long; they formed an almost random heap, like giant spillikins ready for the ancient game of extracting one of them without making the others tremble. I called it 'Autobiography', thinking of the varied pace, weight and unforeseen crisscrossings of the factors of one's life. These rods were painted white with black bands around them; a critic I invited to see them in my studio when they were new thought they looked like 'measure become organic' – as if measuring rods could interbreed. The other collection consisted of thirty-one slender rods, painted white but each having a different inch-long section painted grey; I called it 'Inchworm' as it reminded me of some twig-like geometer caterpillars I kept in a jamjar and who were my silent and usually motionless companions for long hours in my studio at the time I was working on this piece. One could order these rods side by side on the floor so that the grey section appeared to crawl from one end of the collection to the other, but in truth I did not have any particular way of arranging them in mind when they were made (in fact I can't remember making them at all and was surprised when they came to light some ten years later). By the time of the IMMA show I had discovered that if I held them like a vertical sheaf with one end resting on the floor and then let go, they fell apart into a fan-shape, an elegant example of a broken symmetry.

These titles and the significances attached to them

are the work of my wisdom after the event – many years after, in some cases, for these rod-works date from 1971 or so, shortly before our move to Aran. Or perhaps they are the work of my foolishness, for although I admire the rigour of artists who eschew titles and leave the interpretation of their works to the viewer, I cannot forbear to nudge people's attention in the direction of whatever I currently regard as the features that link my works into a net of mutual references. That knitwork, precisely, is what I'm at in the present writing.

So: the 'stride taken towards the centre of the earth' could be the summation of all the strides, steps and paces that mark the progress of my two-volume walk, first around the coast and then in and out of the holes and corners of the interior of Árainn, the largest of the Aran Islands and, as I wrote in *Stones of Aran: Pilgrimage*, 'the exemplary terrain upon which to dream of that work, the guidebook to the adequate step'. The concept of this good step is introduced with the help of dolphins I once watched off an Aran beach, plunging through their element as if they were 'wave made flesh, with minds solely to ensure the moment-by-moment reintegration of body and world'. 'Let the problem be symbolised as taking a single step as adequate to the ground it clears as is the dolphin's arc to its wave'; that is, for us inhabitants of a craggy and multifaceted world, being mindful of its plenitude both physical and social. (For the universe is a mighty small place and we have to make what we can of it.) But by the end of my book's circumambulation of the island I am ready to admit that 'the notion of a momentary congruence between the culture one bears and the ground that bears one has shattered against reality into uncountable fragments, the endless variety of steps that are more or less good enough for one or two aspects of the here and now.' Nevertheless, the step continues to work as an energizing motif throughout the book, and towards the end reveals its secret ambition. Near the end of *Stones of Aran: Labyrinth*, after describing the panic-inducing experience of trying to walk blindfold across one of the island's crevasse-ridden cliff-edged plateaus, I claim to have realized the nature of the step: 'As the foot descends through space, a surface exactly the size and shape of the foot-sole receives it; this support is the top of a column of inconceivable height that goes down and down, narrower and narrower, until it rests upon a point, a nothing, at the centre of the earth, and from that point opens up again in the opposite direction like the cone of futurity opening out of a moment, into the unsoundable.' An attempt, this, at trusting the physical world in its incalculable richness, and a mad ambition to include totality in each contact with it! Perhaps life is too short to accommodate more than one idea. The cone of silk threads opening out from the top of the white rod and embracing whatever room it is hung in was constructed in 1971 or '2, while the passage it seems to illustrate was written in about 1993. That inescapability of one's own stock of mental imagery is the theme of 'The View from the Horizon'.

In fact the suspended rod and its companion works are the skeletal offspring of a time of no ideas, when I had drifted away from the egotistic dynamism of the London art world into a state of aimlessness, in which I fiddled around vacantly with my wooden rods, painting them white with black bands as described above, stacking them in a corner or handing them one by one to the rare visitors to my studio for them to feel the weight and balance of each. (I bought the rods – dowelling rods in a more functional world – very cheaply from a hardware store; I hadn't heard of the Arte Povera artists at that time, but coming across their works since I have been moved by their frugal aesthetic. My 'points', described below in 'The Tale of a Washer', were an even more parsimonious product of this period of apparent sterility, just before our move from London to Aran in 1972.)

The Hugh Lane installation included another element: a set of a dozen ink brushworks on paper depicting winged figures that drew on memories of seeing the majestic Nike of Samothrace, the Greek goddess of victory, in the Louvre. I'll write about their interior provenance later on; here I'll try to justify their inclusion in the minimalist world ruled over by the suspended rod. First, their medium, black ink on white paper, pointed through a decade or more of time to the black-on-white maps I made after our move to Aran, copies of which were also exhibited as part of these installations. But this is a strained linkage; perhaps their form validates their presence better. The bodies of these aerial beings consist of a few sketchy vortices arranged on a vertical axis and are borne up by widespread wings, skeletal but feather-light. The suspended rod with its radiating threads could be seen as a generalized diagram of this gesture, which is one of generosity and joy.

Finally, and as if shyly occupying a place in a corner, the Hugh Lane version of the installation included the 'Ghost Stairs': a score of very slim rods, unpainted, about three feet long and laid out in parallel. In the plank-floored London room in which they were first assembled (in about 1973) they lay in the grooves between successive planks; in the Hugh Lane they were less comfortable on a fishbone-patterned parquet floor. In either setting they suggested an almost imperceptible staircase descending into nothingness: a shadowy, cautionary version of the white signpost to the centre of the earth that ruled over all these manifestations.

4. The Tale of a Washer

In April 1990, after decades of planning and construction, the Hubble Space Telescope was loaded into the cargo hold of a space shuttle and blasted on the back of a rocket to a height of 559 kilometres, where it was put into orbit around the earth. At that height the atmosphere is so tenuous that it does not interfere with the Hubble's view of astronomical objects so faint and far away as to be beyond the ken of all previous telescopes. The heart of the Hubble is a bowl-shaped mirror, nearly eight feet across and polished to within a hundred millionths of a millimetre of a perfect hyperboloid, which collects the light from whatever stars and galaxies lie within its field of view and focuses it on a camera of exquisite sensitivity. The prime purpose of this wonderful construction is to pierce the distances curtaining the birth scene of spacetime itself.

Having followed the space shuttle's blazing ascent, the telescope's successful injection into the correct orbit, the unfurling of its dragonfly wings of solar cells and the initiation of its functions, no doubt the teams of scientists and technicians responsible for various aspects of this technological triumph sat back with a sigh of relief, and waited for the first sublime starscapes to appear on the monitors in the Goddard Space Flight Center. And what did the stars look like? Squashed spiders! So said one astronomer I have seen quoted. An anguished analysis of the blurry images indicated that the great mirror was slightly too flat (by 2.2 thousandths of a millimetre) near its perimeter. Who was to blame? It seems that the error was due to a fault in an optical gadget used to check the curvature of the mirror. In this instrument a certain lens was out of position, by

1.55 mm. Somebody had omitted to insert a washer behind it, it was said.

The Hubble is designed to be serviced in orbit as needs arise, by space-walking technicians tethered to a space shuttle, for the cost of bringing it back to earth for refitting would be prohibitive. Three years after the initial launch a team of seven astronauts, trained in the use of some hundred specialist implements, were space-shuttled up, and over ten days installed a number of optical devices designed to correct the spherical aberration of the primary mirror. The cost of that washer must have mounted into the hundreds of millions of dollars. Since then, however, the Hubble has been an astounding success and still posts home avalanches of information on star formation and many other research topics, and especially on the early history of the universe, the unfurling of time and space.

Such questions interest me deeply, but my wandering mind is as often drawn to a question that has been left behind, being a triviality. What about that washer? Had it slipped from the fingers and then from the memory of some technician harassed by the everyday pressures of life on earth as well as the Hubble project's problems of schedule-slippage and cost-overrun? Did it lie, its glints and gleams unnoticed, on the floor of some 'clean room', until it was swept up and dumped with other waste into a dustbin? Or might some time-ridden space-stepper like myself have noticed it and carried it off as a memento? To work out what role this little disc plays in my own explorations of time and space requires me to revisit a crucial period in my life and that of my partner: 1972, the year of our decision to leave London.

I was at that time given to long wanderings from my base in north-west London, orientating myself by sun and wind, by the rumblings of distant railway lines, and especially by glimpses of the church spires that watch over Kilburn, Cricklewood, Hendon and others of London's ingested but not totally digested villages, which I came to identify with the towers that triangulate Proust's account of a carriage ride in the French countryside, in an essay that inaugurated his literary career. In those walks, roads to me were merely lines of least resistance in the substance of the city I was trying to walk through as if it were wilderness. Vainly, for the sheer extent of the city held my body as on a leash. My mind in turn was tethered to my body, free to drift in blue-blank or tumultuous cloudy skies until occasionally summoned to its function of attention (for experience calls on both body and mind) by the sight of something gleaming on the pavement before me or in the gutter: a little brassy disc, perhaps a button, or a washer mislaid by someone servicing a motorbike or a car. I began to collect these 'points', as I came to term them, trying to commit to memory whatever vague ramblings my mind had reported in that moment of recall, so that by the time I had brought them home they already represented a bygone instant, a 'now' foregone. In an analysis of the act of pointing, a philosopher – I forget who – introduced the concept of 'the point of ostension': the point in which a straight line prolonging the direction of a pointing index finger first meets a solid surface. Remembering this gesture of power, I would pick up the 'point', the washer or button or whatever it was, on the tip of my index finger, add a touch of glue, and by pointing affix it to a wall of my studio. Sometimes then it happened that I would notice a sudden intensification of the gaze of a visitor idly looking around the room and by chance catching – or being caught by – sight of the little star. Or I might give the point to someone, with instructions to throw it away at home, forget about it, come across it by chance after some years, and let me know, if I should still be here to know anything, the exact mental content of the moment of rediscovery. In either scenario I would know that a moment, an instant, had been salvaged from the memory-drowning onrush of time. In reality I never heard back from any recipient of a point, and to be honest I don't positively remember ever handing one over to such a dubious future. Nor do I have any of them now. Perhaps they are still glued to those points of ostension, occasionally remarked upon by some puzzled occupant of the home that once was ours.

For me, these instants, anchor points of evanescent nows, stood for moments of revelation to oneself of one's own existence. Rethinking them now, though, perhaps they represent the not-quite-dimensionless intervals between our mind's experience of past and of future, the allowance made for dawdling nerve signals and redundant neuron-work in such imperfect confections of flesh as we; they fill the gaps in our consciousness of self and world. But in any case, in my imaginary gallery of points pride of place goes to the washer lost in the building of the Hubble telescope. It stands for the first of all moments, separating not past from future but nothing from something; it is the grain from which the universe burst into existence and begat all that is and ever will be. All things stand at ground zero of that explosion; it links us all in a universal cousinage. It is the All-Thing lying in the palm of the mystic, bereft perhaps of maker and sustainer, but not of love.

5. To the Sun, to the Moon

The cut-out pieces of 'Moonfield' and 'Four-Colour Theorem' inherited their shapes from an immediately previous generation of large abstract paintings fed by geography and geometry in equal parts. The geography I found in Provence (but could have found its equivalent elsewhere) in the course of a strenuous and solitary wandering on foot and by lifts, in the summer of 1968; the geometry was invented on my return, in a sudden release of creativity. That historical and magical date, 1968, prompts one to ask why I did not go to Paris where a new mode of social being was struggling to be born; but, sympathetic as I was to *les évènements*, I wanted a way of being of my own, and although it was hardly a matter of physical wellbeing, foot-blistered and way-weary as I was much of the time, I flourished in the empowering sunlight and my freedom to accept whatever lifts were offered, wherever they were headed. I came home with a new series of paintings in my head, or at least their titles: 'To the Sun', 'Windward', etc. These would be thoroughly abstract compositions, answering to my concept of topographical sensations, that is, sensations such as crossing a pass and seeing the lowland beyond open up, completing the circuit of an island, or reaching the summit of an isolated hill – experiences the kernel of which does not depend on the texture of the terrain but solely on its topography.

To give the maximum of room to my visions and make them embrace the viewer, I took to working on big (five- or six-foot square) canvases hung by a corner so as to stress the surprising length of their diagonals. Their surfaces were divided up into two or three shapes, in bright flat colours or white, defined by edges of the canvas and circular arcs of certain radii, calculated to give the shapes some interesting theorem-like interrelations. (These radii were those of the following circles, all somehow maximal in terms of a unit square: the largest circle that can be fitted into the square; the largest quarter-circle that can be fitted into the square; the largest circle that can be fitted into the preceding quarter-circle; the largest circle that can be fitted into a half-square, i.e. a square divided along one of its diagonals.) Because of their diamond-wise hanging these works urged the viewer onwards in one direction or the other, like big road signs, or promoted a balance between opposite impulses.

How few of these canvases survive! – too few to explore the abstract schema underlying them by using all possible combinations of the arcs it defines. However, this clutch of works provided the shapes for the installations that succeeded to them, and no doubt through that line of descent have an affinity with my maps, while the idea of topographical sensations that underlies them makes itself known here and there in writings of much later years. Nevertheless, sometimes I wonder if a thorough exploration of their potentialities could be carried out as a series of black-on-white prints. But perhaps that Orphic backwards glance would just leave them stranded between past and present.

If the mathematico-topological works described above were energized by sunlight, the paintings that immediately preceded them owe a debt to the moon. That series was called 'The Dreams of Euclid', from which one can see that they inhabit some tidal region between the high seas of the irrational and the dry land of reason. I was very interested in, not the meanings so much as the phenomenology of dreams in my early years, when my nights almost capsized under the weight of them. Two sets of prints from that period, 'The Theory and Practice of Dreams', laid out in little panels somewhat like a comic strip, explore the extreme transformations a dream-object can undergo while still being the same thing throughout. 'The Dreams of Euclid' nodded to the same theme, but with a severely limited repertoire of forms.

In several of these oil paintings a square canvas is nearly filled by a four-by-four or five-by-five array of plate-sized circles touching each other edge to edge, with another such array slightly tilted and off-centred relative to the first and nearly eclipsing them, leaving the canvas almost covered by a pattern of sickle moons. In other works of this period single circles or slightly off-circular shapes arrived at by merging two or more overlapping circles occupy most of a square canvas without being exactly centred within it. Near the centres of these floating shapes is a handful of circles hardly bigger than an old penny coin; one might notice that they form a triangular array, or one array superimposed on another; an analytic look, ruler in hand, would find a congruence between these little constellations and the (unmarked) centres of the big circles. Colours: subdued, silvery or greenish grey. Geometry is born of mystery, these works could be understood to say, or mystery is born of geometry. I always took it that they hinted at cosmic processes, but when we resurrected them after the flood and saw them as a group for the first time for decades, M pointed out what then became obvious: these paintings could be seen as tender likenesses of tiny embryos in the tranquillity of a womb. So perhaps mine was a censored and escapist interpretation of them. It would be a breach of privacy to follow this theme further.

6. A Day in Darkness

In March 1963, in the Vienna State Opera House, shortly before a performance of Wagner's *Die Walküre,* the body of a little girl was found in a backstage washroom. She had been stabbed thirty-seven times. The performance went ahead; the corpse was discreetly being removed as the curtain went up. She was aged twelve and she had come to the Opera House to attend a ballet school rehearsal. Her name was Dagmar Fuhrich.

Soon afterwards a man understood (if that is the word) to be a pathological woman-hater, who somehow had gained access to the cavernous labyrinths behind the scene on stage, was arrested, tried and found guilty of the murder of Dagmar. He had only shortly before this event completed a prison sentence for another attack, and he warned the court that he would offend again if released. Sentenced to life imprisonment, he spent forty-one years in virtual isolation before his death in 2004. His name was Josef Weinwurm.

At the time of our settling in Vienna this murder was the talk of the city, of which the glittering and majestic Opera House, bombed out in the War and newly rebuilt, was the cultural crown. We soon heard of an unusual addendum to Weinwurm's sentence: that he was to spend each anniversary of his deed in darkness. When I think of it now, this profound condition – profoundly cruel? profoundly just? – takes me back to Robert Musil's vast, unfinished and perhaps unfinishable novel *The Man Without Qualities*, which sniffs the atmosphere of Vienna just before the First World War. Musil's protagonist is a man of leisure, a flâneur of the intellect who has never committed himself to any activity sustained enough for it to imprint a quality on him, and has even come to envy for his obsessions a certain convicted murderer, a wise simpleton who had stabbed to death a young prostitute he felt was forcing herself on him. This shy itinerant carpenter, who inflicted thirty-five wounds in the girl's belly and otherwise horribly mutilated her, is in prison pending a decision on whether he is insane or not, and so to be hanged or not. A net to catch the shadow-side of the city could, I feel, be strung between Musil's pathetic wanderer and the man of annual darkness of our days in Vienna.

However, I cannot blame the city for the streak of darkness that runs through me and is amply revealed by the black-ink paintings I produced during our three years in Vienna; that has been there from the beginning, memory says, and I have no intention of playing Freud about it in this context. But the most disturbing or disturbed of these paintings might well have caught up their explicit content from the Opera House murder, for they represent monsters – solitary creatures, powerful, malignant, almost brainless, pitiable in their bestiality, prowling shadowy tunnels. A related series of black-ink paintings, 'Cities in a Vacuum', features towering, windowless buildings aligned by a ruthless perspective on a diseased sun – cities so perfect that my monsters can only peer out at them from sewers or crack-like alleys. Here perhaps I was influenced by a sinister component of the architecture of Vienna, in which the huge grim concrete cuboid of a bomb-shelter left over from the Hitler days, and the endlessly long fortress-like blocks of workers' apartments, Karl Marx-Hof and Friedrich Engels-Hof, which once housed rebellion and had been shelled in the time of the proto-Nazi dictator Dollfuss, counted for more than all the pompous palaces of the Ringstrasse.

Rather less literal than these paintings, which could be illustrations of unwritten science fictions, were some large ink drawings of beings that look as if they might have evolved into humans had they not half-metamorphosed into leafless birch trees with broken-off branches. (These multiply castrated entities can I think be traced back to a dreary grey-green painting dating from my late teens, a face-on view of three or four pollarded trees raising their fists behind the railings of a featureless municipal park. I now read this early work as a symptom of small-town claustrophobia, a longing for an Elsewhere of cultural, social and sexual delights.)

Allied to these tree-men works are some drawings of half-skeletonized birds falling out of a layered grey sky; I thought of these creatures as having been slain in mid-air by a blast of atomic radiation. My Armageddon fantasies caught the uneasy mood of Vienna; the Russian army had pulled out of our section of the city only seven or eight years previously, and we soon found out that our neighbours were very cagey about their lives in the decade of occupation before that exodus. The frontier between East and West was only fifty kilometres away; defecting artists were made welcome by organizations funded by, it was said, the CIA. Café society was rumoured to be riddled with spies, so that if two intellectuals sat down to found a new movement they would soon find that two strangers had joined them, the spy from the East and the spy from the West. At the crux of the Cold War, when an American spy plane detected Russian nuclear missiles installed in Cuba, daily life, work, love and laughter went on regardless, but something in our minds held its breath. Around that time I was drawing bombers that burst through windows and walls and loomed over loving couples reduced to tangled anxieties. Also I came across a photograph of the Statue of Liberty under construction, a giant skeleton from which ant-sized humans dangled on threads; this suggested a set of twelve small ink drawings done on damp paper, in which the talismanic statue is trans-mogrified into surreal and sadistic contraptions of metal fangs and squashy entrails, and finally dissolves into night and fog.

I don't remember that any of these works were done with conscious ideological intent; they grew obscurely but naturally out of the mud of contemporary events. In the end and quite mysteriously, not in response to any amelioration of worlds interior or exterior that I know of, my rampant monsters, as if they had coupled with my falling birds, gave rise to a joyous brood of winged creatures. These light-as-air beings were suggested by the Nike of Samothrace, imagined as about to take off from her glorious stance on the grand staircase of the Louvre, her lopped wings regrown. These calligraphic ink drawings were each summoned into existence in a couple of minutes with a few whirls and swipes of a wide flat brush, in a win-all lose-all mode; about a dozen of them survived the risks of their birth. Looking at them recently I was struck by a feature that had not been salient to me when they were new: their bodies are made up of two halves in close embrace, each with one wing. They remind me of Apollinaire's mythical Chinese bird, the Pihi, which has only one wing and flies in couples – and so they bring me a happy memory of my first rapturous encounter with French poetry. I take this bird-flight of good augury as an emblem of my awakening from the long dark day of Vienna.

7. Juvenilia

Under this title I sweep together all the artwork done before I turned down an invitation to continue in my teaching post in Istanbul, declared myself (to myself) to be a painter, and moved to Vienna. Looking at the works that survive from time that would have been better spent on getting to know my pupils in Robert College, on my mathematical studies in Cambridge, on servicing the radar devices entrusted to me as an RAF technician in Malaya, or on my homework from Ilkley Grammar School, and so on back to the war-inspired drawings of my primary school days, I see first a glaring lack of talent. Then, here and there in those childhood sketch-books, so proudly preserved by my parents, I make out a flicker of merit — in fanciful drawings of Flying For-tresses (a new development in aerial warfare we learned about from newspapers, and which I took to be airborne castles with parapets and towers), in a meticulous series of images of butterfly wings earnestly copied from one of the natural history books I pored over as a teenager, or in diagrams of the dozens of different knots that seemed to obsess the Boy Scout movement.

Among the earliest surviving sketches, alongside numerous drawings of tank battles, Tarzan wrestling wild beasts, etc., there are some scenes in visionary or lyric mode. In one of these a child is led by the hand through a wood by a hooded, monkish figure, who indicates with a rapturous gesture the birdsong, represented as huge bubbles, tumbling out of the trees; the child imitates his gesture. This sketch seems to express a need for a protector or mentor, for although my parents were supportive of my artistic effort they would not have followed me into the magical world of surrealism, and nor would our vicar, a family friend, have had much time for my budding pantheism. Some paintings of my early teens express the same mood. In one of them a serene, classically naked, male figure, seen from the back, gazes out of an opening in some structure of stone blocks at a sky in which eleven moons are shown in various phases and settings. Another is an attempt to convey the sensation of drowsing in summer heat; a pair of hands – the viewer's hands as seen from inches away – frames the entrance to a tunnel that opens onto the night sky on the other side of the world.

As if to counterbalance these reflective and peaceable works there are some nightmares, some spasms of anxiety, dating from the same period. In a small watercolour titled 'Doctor Comforting a Patient', the doctor is an imperturbably massive cubist figure, while the patient is a ragged streak of pain, angular as a lightning flash, lying across him. A rather ambitious, would-be photo-realist oil painting features a man, who could be a corpse, in nondescript uniform, lying among strands of barbed wire; his clenched fists occupy the foreground, and there is fire and wreckage in the distance. Another seems to be a reminiscence of Dante: a huge three-headed dog leads a chain-gang of miserable captives down an avenue of trees in which are hanging strange creatures consisting of hands growing out of trunkless heads. A small scraperboard work perhaps inspired by Dostoevsky shows the face and arms of a mad axe-man seen close-up and from the point of view of his victim; when this came to light recently M immediately spotted it as the origin of the monstrous semi-human denizens of my Viennese paintings of a dec-ade later. Thus my taking myself seriously as an artist began with abrupt alternations of strange but reassuring worlds and abyssal depths of suffering. But let me not fan-tasize about what these works might have been had they not been so gauche in execution; I mention them only to complete this sketch of half a lifetime's essays in visual art, and to hint at a fruitful self-contradiction I find in much subsequent work.

One strand of this awkward development is worth separating out from the tangles of adolescence. It shows itself in some oils in villainous colour-schemes done in Cambridge, and in almost decorative pen-and-ink illustrations published in the undergraduate magazines of those days. They have a common form or contradiction of forms: a rectangular grid of lines supports or transfixes a lyrical effusion of flamelike or leaflike shapes. The origins of the grid I can place: it derives from the systems of coordinates I was learning about in connection with the various geometries, Euclidian, projective, Riemannian, etc., that were for me the most fascinating subjects of my maths degree course. And the freeform creations flitting through them like storm-torn sails fighting to rip themselves away from masts and rigging, or like jungle growth overwhelming ancient ruins, originated in my ecstatic encounter with Ayudhia, the deserted former capital of Siam, on one of the most exciting days of my life, during my spell of conscription in Malaya. The individual paintings and drawings of this sort are not worth much in themselves, but they undoubtedly underlie the bipolar nature of my subsequent work, not only in visual art but in cartography and literature too. If reason and unreason, ecstasy and melancholy, go hand in hand in all that I have done, so it was from my beginning.

8. Unrealized Projects

Why now revert to projects abandoned when we made the life-defining move from London to the Aran Islands in 1972? Because at the moment I am battering myself against the same impenetrable void that surrounded me in my West Hampstead studio in those pre-transition days, and they dimly come into view again with a vague promise of release. So it might be a healing exercise to reconsider them in the light or dark of passing years. What were they? Why were they not brought into existence? How is it that some of them seem to pre-echo the Aran literary and topographical work? What do they propose for the present moment? Their names still speak to me:

Exploding mirror
Deadly environments and critic traps
Spots of time
The wavy floor
Ring and cube
Resistance
Arabidopsis

Exploding Mirror

Place a mirror face down on a bed of sand in a shallow open-topped box or drawer. Drop a stone onto the middle of its back so that the front surface of the mirror, now broken up into shards, bulges down into the sand. Remove the stone and spread the back of the mirror with a layer of concrete or plaster to fix the shards in place. When this has hardened remove the mirror from the box and wash any adherent sand off its face.

I imagine that the result would look like a frozen instant in an explosion behind the mirror, or of something, perhaps a mirror image, in the act of breaking out of the mirror world into reality. Words written a couple of decades later inadvertently say something about the mental state that gave rise to this proposed work. In *Setting Foot on* the Shores of Connemara I liken the multitude of lakes of Roundstone Bog, as seen from a neighbouring hilltop, to 'fragments of a mirror flung down and shattered'. And in *Connemara: Listening to the Wind*, describing the mood of this same landscape, I write that the adjective that came spontaneously to my mind was 'frightened':

> For a moment I felt I had identified the force that drives the expansion, the self-scattering, of the universe: fear. The outline of each lake bristles with projections, every one of which is itself spiny; they stab at one another blindly. There is a fractal torment animating the scene, which is even more marked in aerial photographs, in which the lakes seem to fly apart like shrapnel. Of course all this is purely subjective and projective: I was the only frightened element of the situation . . .

So I can take it that fear, and therefore aggression, underlies the erupting, image-shattering, mirror that never saw the light. Since mine is the reflection I would be most likely to see if the project had been realized, the broken mirror correctly anticipates my sense of myself today.

Deadly Environments and Critic Traps

I reawaken these works from nothingness with reluctance, as they so obviously spring from some short-lived malignity towards the world of art. To quote from a let's pretend review of which a faded typescript draft has drifted down to the present:

'The Lethal Environment'. Lisson Gallery
The cellar of the Lisson Gallery this month is given over to an unwelcome development in environmental art. Jagged sheets of broken glass, some of them four or five feet long, project from the walls, floor and ceiling, leaving a tunnel just about big enough to creep along. The glass spikes are smeared with a bluish phosphorus rat-poison.

I seem to detect a certain rancour in the artist's relation to his audience here, in that the word 'environment' appears to be an invitation to experience this work of art from within, which would of course be fatal. I am not convinced that the death of some middle-aged art critic would help to heal the breach between Society and the Artist: and, indeed, so far no one has volunteered the sacrifice. Viewed from outside, of course, the dazzling tracery formed by the edges of the bits of glass, suffused by the vaporous blue tones of the rat poison, produce an effect which is, to put it bluntly, beautiful. However, that may not be the point.

The critic traps thankfully were never constructed or even written about; they were little devices from which a coiled spring sharp as a razor flashed out at any viewer who bent to inspect their ingenuity closely. They presumably date from the period of my (on the whole amicable) connection with the Lisson Gallery, but I do not remember any incident that might have led me to conceive them. I mention them here for completeness, but they would be better forgotten.

Spots of Time

Rods and washers, two sorts of works from the time of my dwindling presence in the London art world have been written up separately, but perhaps a joint consideration of both would be productive. And since the washers did not literally have to be washers but any little discs found lying on a pavement, say, that might arrest the eye and give rise to memorable 'spots of time' (a famous and curious phrase I came across in labouring through Wordsworth recently), they could even be manufactured by cutting thin cross-sections from one of the more slender rods.

If these cross-sections of the rods are taken to mark 'spots of time' then the rods as wholes can be seen as chronometers of imaginary time-dimensions. Produced one by one out of agonies of boredom, most of the rods were painted with regularly spaced bands of black on a white ground, and when they were casually stacked away in a corner could sometimes be imagined as ticking away to themselves.

The washers are on my mind these days because of the unexpected and partly inexplicable appearance of one stuck to a wall in the Royal Academy, together with a framed text derived from my account of the Hubble telescope and the washer rumoured to have been omitted in its construction. In my days as a radical aesthete I would have regarded the RA as the enemy, but change is the only constant in this world and I was as flattered as I was surprised to be invited by the architect Ian Ritchie to exhibit a work in the 2015 Summer Show. He overrode my protests that it was many a year since I had produced any visual work, and undertook to frame and hang the text himself and affix a washer near it – all of which came to pass (and then somebody bought the work, for £150, on the show's opening day, despite the fact that the washer was superglued to Burlington House).

While I have made no profit from the discovery of washers (or points, as I prefer to call them), I keep an eye on the possibility of creating them cheaply and merchandizing them in bulk. However, this remains an unrealized project. First, the creative leap. Take a sheaf of rods of the required diameter and composition, and shave off the uneven ends. Then use some mechanical device to advance the sheaf by whatever thickness is required for the sort of points you have in mind, and shave off that much as before (say 1.25 mm for a washer).

A golden shower of these precious shapes can now be expelled from your machine as convenient, their number expressible only in Wordsworthian ten-thousands.

The Wavy Floor

My article in the *Bulletin of the Computer Arts Society*, February 1971, refers to this project as 'Field Work 3: A Structured Arena'. Most of the article was given over to the mathematics of the thing, illustrated with my elegant little diagrams. I was very proud of the mathematics, although to a real mathematician it would be child's play, and of my diagrams, which take me back to the period in which I worked as a part-time freelance technical illustrator. Both calculations and illustrations would be beyond me now. I copy the beginning of the text:

> Last year [1969 in fact] I showed two environmental works in London involving a large degree of participation ['Four-colour Theorem', in Kenwood House kitchen garden, and 'Moonfield', in Camden Arts Centre]. Watching people react to these, I became less interested in the transient results of their activities, and more aware of the way in which those activities were themselves patterned by the structure of what I had provided. That is, I stopped thinking of these works as 'participational' (as delegating a certain range of

aesthetic decision); instead I began to see the actions of those involved as the object of my activity as an artist. This led me to think of creating areas that would impose certain rhythms on anything taking place within them, and on the consciousness of anyone entering them. One project I considered was a concrete floor of regularly-spaced shallow waves, perhaps four inches high and just over a stride from top to top: the area covered would be large enough for a specific rhythm to be generated by the act of walking across it. This floor would not be presented as a finished artwork, but as an arena for experiment by myself or anyone else. It would be interesting to try different lighting effects, for example: a strong overhead lighting, with the floor painted white, would make the surface difficult to 'read' as one walked over it; illumination by a flickering candle down in one corner would turn it into a sea of pulsating shadows. Again, people could explore it and discover its structure by touch, in complete darkness.

On this continuously curved surface one could experiment with discontinuous 'additions'; a scattering of rigid, fragile 'measuring rods' would change its character; balls would bounce on it unpredictably; various amounts of water would convert it into a series of ponds, and then into a series of islands. Musical, dance or theatrical groups could let the rhythms of their own activities interact with its periodic structure. In general the interest would lie in the 'interference' of the floor's stable and coherent wave-structure, with the unstable and fluctuating forms of action superimposed on it.

A rectangular array of waves would probably be my final choice, but when considering a triangular array I became interested in the mathematics of the situation: this is another approach to comprehending it as a structure . . .

. . . And having explored this other approach and incidentally invented a function that 'represents a network of triangles turning itself inside out to form other networks of triangles, in a three-stage cycle', I ended my paper by hoping that a proper mathematician might investigate what underlies this function, and that I would some day see it realized in a wave-tank, 'or if possible as a computer graphic display' – a phrase that reminds me how long ago all this was.

Obviously the concrete floor project has its connections with the other floorworks ('Four-colour Theorem' and 'Moonscape') of 1969, and in all three a dim premonition is to be glimpsed of the development and abandonment of the concept of the good step, which was suggested by a sight of dolphins plunging through waves. *Stones of Aran: Pilgrimage* is all made up of steps and leads one on a walk around the perimeter of the island; I quote from two stages in the evolution of the trope:

Let the problem be symbolized by that of taking a single step as adequate to the ground it clears as is the dolphin's arc to its wave. Is it possible to think towards a human conception of this 'good step'? . . . But our world has nurtured in us such a multiplicity of modes of awareness that it must be impossible to bring them to a common focus even for the notional duration of a step. The dolphin's world, for all that its inhabitants can sense Gulf Streams of diffuse beneficences, freshening influences of rivers and perhaps a hundred other transparent gradations, is endlessly more continuous and therefore productive of unity than ours, our craggy, boggy, overgrown and overbuilt terrain, on which every step carries us across geologies, biologies, myths, histories, politics, etcetera, and trips us with the trailing *Rosa spinosissima* of personal associations. To forget these dimensions of the step is to forgo our honour as human beings, but an awareness of them equal to the involuted complexities under foot at any given moment would be a crushing backload to have to carry. Can such contradictions be forged into a state of consciousness even fleetingly worthy of its ground? At least one can speculate that the structure of condensation and ordering necessary to pass from such various types of knowledge to such an instant of insight would have the characteristics of a work of art, partaking of the individuality of the mind that bears it, yet with a density of content and richness of connectivity surpassing any state of that mind. So the step lies beyond a certain work of art; it would be like a reading of that work. And the writing of such a work? Impossible, for many reasons, of which the brevity of life is one.

[. . .]

The notion of a momentary congruence between the culture one bears and the ground that bears one has shattered against reality into uncountable fragments, the endless variety of steps that are more or less good enough for one or two aspects of the here and now. These splinters might be put together into some more serviceable whole by paying more heed to their cumulative nature, to the step's repeatability, variability, reversibility and expendability. The step, so mobile, so labile, so nimbly coupling place and person, mood and matter, occasion and purpose, begins to emerge as a metaphor of a certain way of living on this earth. It is a momentary proposition put by the individual to the non-individual, a not-quite infallible catching of oneself in the act of falling . . . With this freebooter's licence goes every likelihood of superficiality, restlessness, fickleness – and so, by contraries, goes the possibility of recurrency, of frequentation, of a deep, an ever-deeper, dwelling in and on a place, a sum of whims and fantasies totalling a constancy as of stone.

Stone, of course, is the other structuring metaphor in *Stones of Aran*, and indeed it is the dominating reality of life on the island. It was the bareness of Aran limestone, the legibility of its fossils and ruins, its prehistory and history, that suggested the possibility of mapping it. Hence the actual landscape of the islands reminds one of the floorworks, which have features in common with both landscapes and maps. No need to pursue this theme; it is salient in all the books. Instead I turn to a question that occurs to me now:

Why was this so-called 'wavy floor' to be made of concrete? Wood or some sort of plastic would be just as feasible, and less abrasive if anyone should fall on this surface, which seems designed to trip one up. I don't remember looking into this question at the time. Perhaps the answer lies in the word and its associations. Taken adjectivally, 'concrete' means existing in material form, in reality as opposed to the abstract. So it has connotations of fixity and solidity – whereas all the possible additions to the basic structure I suggest – light and shadow, measuring rods, bouncing balls, water – are temporary, changeable, unpredictable, unstable. A gallery exhibiting the wavy floor would probably stipulate that dancers venture onto it only at their own risk, whereas in my paper quoted above mathematicians are invited to de-reify it and establish its abstract features by process of proof.

Risk and proof, maths and the imagination, structure and freedom – somewhere near here is buried the binary opposition that has informed my creative life.

Ring and Cube

Having used various maximal circular arcs in the direc-
tional paintings of 1968, I began to think about
three-dimensional equivalents. What is the diameter of
the largest circle that can be fitted into a cube? The
answer, in terms of the length of a side of the cube, is
$\sqrt{(3/2)}$ – but that's no matter except to the numerical
chatterbox mind. Choose a vertex of the cube, and a
pair of sides that meet in it. Join the midpoints of these
two sides by a line (A). Do the same starting from the
vertex opposite to the first one, and the pair of sides
opposite to the first pair, to produce a line (B). A and B
are parallel. Slice through them both with a plane bisect-
ing the cube. The cut face of one of the half-cubes is
hexagonal. Inscribe a circle in this hexagon, touching
the midpoints of all six sides of it. Since the sides of the
hexagon each lie on a face of the cube, the circle touches
each of the cube's six faces and if it were any larger would
exceed the limits of the cube. So it is the largest circle
that can be inscribed in the cube.

To exhibit this construction I envisaged a cubic room,
say twenty-five feet in length, breadth and height, and a
circle in the form of a ring made of tubing a few inches
in cross-section. I calculate that a ring of diameter 30' 6"
would just fit into it so as to touch each of the four walls,
the ceiling and the floor, allowing an inch or two for the

ring's thickness. The room was to be white, the ring blood-red. There was to be an entrance door in the corner of the room nearest to which the ring rests on the floor, and an exit door opposite the entrance, so that anyone who entered would have to step through the ring to exit. Immediately outside the entrance door a silent attendant without explanation would hand each visitor a minute replica of the ring, of the same red and about half an inch in diameter. Only one person at a time would be admitted.

What is this about? The solitariness of the traverse, the enigmatic bestowal of the little ring (which many people might hold in their palm during their visit), suggest ritual, though once inside no particular action is prescribed apart from stepping through the ring, which is a near geometrical necessity. Perhaps a thought of cosmos and microcosmos is at play here. The individual is allotted certain bodily and mental characteristics by the accidents of birth, and has no choice but to make his or her way through an equally unchosen world to death. A clue to the way is that we and the universe are of the same stuff.

Resistance

What happens to a light bulb in the jaws of a vise when the current is switched on? I never had the nerve to try this in practice, but let us take it that if the bulb is very gently held initially it will not explode when illuminated, or at least not immediately. I pictured the vise as mounted on a small work-bench, with the bulb attached to a length of flex hanging from the ceiling above it. This assemblage was to be towards the back wall of a small cell and could be viewed by one or two visitors at a time from the cell's low doorway. Since the conception came to me shortly after the exhibition of my 'Four-colour Theorem' in the gardens of Kenwood, I thought of siting it in a cell-like recess under the tall classical portico of Kenwood House itself; I imagined that there would be access to the door of the cell from a narrow basement area. The contrast between this cramped and dingy underground space and the proud four-pillared portico above it appealed to me. However, I never even got around to ascertaining that there was such a space under the portico.

The cell and the naked bulb put one in mind of Gestapo torture chambers as seen in films; the persistence of the light in shining in such a place of moral darkness directs one to the legend of the French Resistance. But to title the work 'Resistance' would perhaps be too coercive; there is more to be deciphered in it than its obvious connotations. It could also be seen as casting rays of darkness on some seemingly purely formal paintings of that time and earlier. Consider the sphere of the light bulb and the parallel jaws of the vise holding it: this entails the geometry of the largest circle in the cube. In fact all the paintings and floor-works consisting of geometrical shapes based on maximal circles can be seen in the cruel light of 'Resistance' as preservation of space under pressure.

Arabidopsis

Arabidopsis thaliana is the Latin name of the common weed, thale cress. It is an undistinguished-looking little plant, straggling to ten or so inches in height, with small white four-petalled flowers and inch-long tubular seed cases. It is very easy to grow, sets seed prolifically, and is ideal for genetic studies. Its cells each have five chromosomes bearing a total of 27,000 genes, which is a small number for a plant.

A chromosome is a molecule of DNA, and consists of two strands spiralling around each other. Each strand has a long row of molecules called bases running along it. These are of four different types, abbreviated as C, G, A and T; their function was mentioned in 'Byzantium'. Because of their different shapes an A on one strand of the chromosome fits together with a T on the other strand, while a C fits together with a G. The genes consist of segments of the sequence of such base pairs along a chromosome, and the totality of these sequences constitutes the genome. In a human cell there are about 3.2 billion base pairs; in a thale cress cell there are about 127 million. Nowadays such sequences can be read and recorded, by means of powerful, complex and ever-advancing techniques.

In December 2000 the journal *Nature* announced the first virtually complete sequencing of a plant genome, that of thale cress, a task that had occupied an international collaboration of scientists, the Arabidopsis Genome Initiative, since 1996. The sequences of the plant's five chromosomes were published in separate issues of the journal. This was a crucial step on the way to a complete sequencing of the much larger human genome, achieved in 2003. These matters are central to the question of what life is and how it transmits itself from generation to generation; the sequences of bases along the genes encode the instructions for the building of hundreds of different proteins from simpler chemicals, and it is the proteins that carry out the life-functions of the cells.

What first struck me about the thale cress genome as published was its incomprehensibility. Page after dense page of polysyllabic terminology and cryptic diagrams – I relished the general appearance, the message of which is that reality is endlessly more complex than investigation at any given level can reveal. I would like to blow up dozens of pages from the *Nature* articles and paper the walls of a gallery room with them, and in the middle of this room, this blizzard of information, place a small flower-stand bearing a specimen – an individual – of *Arabidopsis,* in a jamjar.

The Arabidopsis project – my proposed artwork,

not the work of the scientists – had reached this point of consideration when I noticed that the abbreviated base names A, C and G, endlessly recurring in the transcribed sequences of base pairs, could be read as musical notes in the octave CDEFGAB. Moreover T could be taken to represent an F three octaves higher. So a sequence of bases spells out a tune, or at least a series of notes. How long would it take to play the entire genome, at, say, a rattling rate of four bases per second? If my calculation is correct, about a year. And if we had a loudspeaker at one end of the room playing the sequence of bases on one strand of a chromosome, there could be another loudspeaker at the other end of the room playing the complementary sequence.

The biomechanism plagiarized by the above project is only a small part of the apparatus by which proteins are built according to the instructions encoded in the base sequences. One could musicalize, or at least tonalize, the workings of this apparatus too, with some ingenuity, adhering to the principle that every note or chord is to be determined by the rules of the musicalization, not by aesthetics or any other source of values. One wants the bare clatter or chatter of creation, the rap of molecule on molecule.

And in the middle of the room, a specimen of the thing itself, in all its modest oddity, its asymmetry, its bending before the slings and arrows of plant-existence.

A Land Without Shortcuts

This essay was written in 2010–11, and delivered as the Parnell Lecture at Magdalene College, Cambridge, in February 2011. It is published here in its original form.

To be summoned to Cambridge from nether Connemara to deliver the Parnell Lecture was a surprise – honorific, but alarming. What to bring, from that famous far-off land? Well, it seems I can begin with good news: The West of Ireland has at last discovered its reason for existing. As you know, Connemara is the land of cloud-shadows drifting across mountainsides. Roundstone, the little fishing and tourist village I live in, is, I claim, the world capital of rainbows. And it has now been discovered that cloud-shadows can be strip-mined, that rainbows can be smelted. For clouds and rain are symptoms of weather, the almost continuous succession of cyclones coming in from the Atlantic, bringing powerful winds, towering waves. Their energy has been going to waste for millions of years, but now it can be tapped; the technology exists, or soon will.

But the trouble with wind energy is that it is not reliably there when you want it. The answer is pumped water storage. Use the electricity from forests of wind turbines and shoals of wave energy converters to pump seawater up into reservoirs in the mountains, and at times of peak demand let it flow down again through generators. And where could one find a landscape better adapted to this grand scheme? In the west of Ireland we have mountains with high glacial valleys, easily dammed, close to an oceanic coastline. These gifts of nature mean that Ireland could not only fuel its own homes and factories but sell the surplus to Europe, exported through a network of pylons and powerlines. All this will be unpolluting, greenhouse-gas-free, a noble and profitable Irish contribution to saving the world. An enterprise boldly calling itself 'Spirit of Ireland' is working out the details even now.

In expressing my horror at this vision of the future, I don't want to sound like a climate-change sceptic. The globe is warming; we are facing into an era of floods, fires, famines; little doubt about it. The Intergovernmental Panel on Climate Change is 95 per cent certain that this is due to human activity. But even if the IPCC authorizes as it were a 5 per cent duty-free allowance of scepticism, I will not avail of it. There is of course intense technical argumentation over the viability of green-energy schemes. But let me take the most sanguine view of them, together with the most anguished view of the environmental crux that seems to make them necessary.

The question is, how much of the world do we have to spoil in order to save it? Must we accept armies of jerkily gesticulating giants on our windswept western hills, perpetually drawing attention to themselves, interrupting the flow of horizons, imposing a large common factor of sameness on wonderfully varied landscapes?

The businesses that are set to profit out of a great leap forward in the mechanization of the countryside enjoy a ready justification in terms of energy crises to come. Is there no arguing with their commodification of wilderness's last refuges? A few years ago I flew out to the Aran Islands to participate in a debate on a proposed windfarm there. On the same flight was a vigorous young enthusiast from an alternative technologies firm. When we extricated ourselves from the cramped little flying pram of an aeroplane and stretched ourselves in the island breeze, which carried a thousand miles of ocean and a million wildflowers to our nostrils, he sniffed it and said with delectation, 'Ah! Kilowatt-hours!' We have a so-called Green Party in Ireland devoted to this alternative technology. Seeing it thundering down the road towards us, the alternative seems to be a choice between two ditches. For the claim that these new modes of energy production are unpolluting is false. Leaving aside the unavoidable pollution caused by their manufacture, transport, installation and decommissioning, they are through their powerful presence grossly disruptive of our aesthetic, corporeal and affective relationships with the earth. The most obvious component of this loss is that where they go, no one else can go. They mean locked gates, culverted streams, barbed wire, forgone hillsides. These are the spoil-heaps of wind-mining.

How widely applicable are the arguments, or rather the persuasions, I am advancing? Do they stand only on territories comparable in their rare beauty and interest to the ones I have chosen to live amongst, or are there less prestigious areas that could well be turned over to windfarms? Let no word of mine undermine the stance of those who would defend some superficially unre-markable or already depleted landscape of which they love certain elusive moods and secret places. But I will write in terms of what I know; and let what generalities emerge find their welcome where they can. It has been my joy and privilege over the last third of a century to explore in great detail, to map and to write about three exceptional landscapes – the Aran Islands, the Burren and Connemara – and I will describe a place from each, in search of the qualities we cherish and should protect. Now one might say, 'But surely these famous landscapes are already protected? Is not the Burren a proposed UNESCO World Heritage site?' Well, recently a commercial concern was wooing the people of the Burren with a scheme for pumped seawater storage in a lovely upland valley near Black Head. The idea was not well received locally, and at present planning permission for such a drastic intervention would be hard to obtain – but we are only at the beginning of the alternative industrial revolution as yet, and the statutory designations of parts of these districts as Special Areas of Protection, National Heritage Areas, Geo-parks and so on could someday be swept aside. There are already three wind turbines towering over the otherwise uninterrupted network of ancient field walls on the uninhabited Atlantic side of Inis Meáin in the Aran Islands, constantly crossing themselves as if to ward off the haunting loneliness of the place. And Connemara is repeatedly probed by would-be windfarm developers, who have had a major success recently on its eastern periphery. But I'll not continue with the environmentalist plaint; in fact all I've said so far is just a few swipes of the machete to get me into the centre of the thicket: the nature of place, what makes a place out of a locality, what makes a place so precious that we feel called upon to protect it in the teeth of all rational argumentation.

The Aran Islands first, and in particular the largest of them, Árainn, where I lived in the 1970s. The three islands are fragments of a single limestone escarpment stretching across the mouth of Galway Bay; the villages keep their heads down out of the gales on the north-eastern slopes of the ridge, and on the exposed Atlantic-facing side of the ridge is a literally amazing landscape of stone walls enclosing tiny plots of rough grazing, some of them much overgrown with brambles, some of them hardly more than sheets of bare limestone, their crevices filled with flowering herbs. This side of the island, Na Craga, the crags, is not much visited since farming on the islands is a fading way of life. So the boreens and róidíní, the narrow stone-walled paths that wriggle through this maze of fields, are crammed with vegetation. Everywhere, in the spring, are paradisal visions of wildflowers; in my first years there I was drunk on flowers, on the nectar of their names. One day in the course of making my map of the islands I was in an unfrequented quarter like this looking for a ruined church I had heard of, one of the many early Christian remains of the islands, nameless and unvisited and abandoned to hazel scrub. A few generations ago, I had been told, an old man called Colm Citte had been passing this way, and had heard the sound of someone churning milk. But he was on his way to Mass, and didn't stop to investigate; he would have been frightened of the fairies in any case. All these places are haunted by half-forgotten folktales. The area I am describing now is called Clochán an Airgid, the stone hut of the money, or the silver; there is a clochán, an early Christian beehive-shaped hut, which has been reduced to its foundations by treasure hunters following the hint of a legend. Later I wrote about the treasure I found that day, in my book *Stones of Aran*:

As I was crossing the field to the ruins of the church, as obscure as everything else on this occult hillside, I heard through the whispering of the still summer afternoon something that could have been Colm Citte's otherworldly churning. Falling water is so rare on Na Craga that I did not identify the sound until I saw a recess under a little scarp at the back of the field, in which silvery drops were cascading through fronds of maidenhair fern and making them tremble continuously. Around this lovely spring were more wildflowers than I had ever gathered in a single glance. On one side of it was a small hawthorn bush with honeysuckle and meadow pea climbing through it, and a lemon-yellow spire of agrimony below, while on the other a tutsan leaned forward to display its flame-coloured berries. Brooklime was growing in the shadow behind the fern-leaves, and the other flowers of damp pastures – purple loosestrife, yellow pimpernel, silverweed – mingled with the meadow flowers at my feet – purple clover, kidney-vetch, meadow buttercup, tormentil, birdsfoot trefoil. The stonier slope above the well assembled the flora of the crags at the level of my eyes: burnet rose, bloody cranesbill, mountain everlasting, milkwort, quaking grass, the tiny squinancywort, the last of the early purple orchids and the first of the common spotted orchids, all with a minutely delicate interweaving of fairy flax. Along the foot of the scarp beside the well I could see wild strawberry, scarlet pimpernel, sanicle, the elegant St John's wort. There were tall mulleins flowering on the top of the slope, and tway-blades in the shadow of the thickets around the ruin.

The band of grey limestone above the well gave it the solemnity of an altar, around which the plants were gathered, each in the colours of its faith. What truth, distilled moment by moment from the rock, was held in perpetual reservation in the dark cup below? The church behind me, brought to its knees among penitential thorns, attended humbly upon the priestcraft of water.

Re-reading this some fifteen years later, I'm surprised by the salience of the religious terminology. I have no faith, no supernaturalist beliefs; so I must re-examine this. I'll return to the question later.

Strangely, Aran presents this precious conformation of place in three locations, or even more. The reason for this generosity is geological. The island chain is carved out of alternating horizontal strata of limestone and shale – sedimentary rocks laid down in the bed of an ocean that fluctuated in depth over millions of years, the limestone representing times when the water was deep and pure, the shale those when it was shallow and muddy. A central date in this period would be about 325 million years ago. Many millions of years later, huge slow earth movements lifted the stacked-up consolidated sediments above sea level, fracturing the brittle limestone, and exposed them to wind, frost, rain and ice. On the Atlantic-facing coast the waves have licked out the soft shale bands, causing the limestone strata above them to collapse, and so carving sheer or overhanging cliffs.

Less abrupt forces of erosion have shaped the more sheltered north-east-facing slopes into a series of broad terraces separated by inland cliffs or scarps ten to twenty feet high. These scarps run along the island chain like contour lines; they each have a stratum of shale usually a few feet deep at their bases, and a thicker stratum of limestone above that. All rainwater quickly sinks through the fractured limestone until it reaches an impervious layer of shale, which channels it horizontally to the foot of one of the little inland scarps, where it bubbles out in springs. Then, spilling out onto the limestone of the terrace below the scarp, it sinks from sight again, only to reappear at the foot of the next scarp, and so on until it reaches the sea. Each of these scarps has a characteristic profile. So the situation I have described, with falling water in a dark recess at the foot of the scarp, a horizontal band of limestone above that, and then a broken slope leading up a few feet to the terrace above, is repeated here and there along the course of the scarp almost from one end of the island to the other.

I remember in particular one of my favourite places, reached by walking along a grand level terrace of almost bare limestone behind the house we lived in; it is called An Poll i bhFolach, the hole in hiding. It is most secretively wrapped away in a tiny enclosure between a crooked loop of drystone wall and a nook of the scarp rising from the rock-terrace. A narrow stile in the wall admits one to this fane, or one can scramble down into it from the slopes above by means of a few steps cut into the scarp face. The water lies in a rough stone-lined hollow, reflecting many of the flowers I noted at Clochán an Airgid. This 'hole in hiding' has the apparent self-regard of a place little visited; it welcomes one, then waits for one to go. But human industry has intensified its mode of being: there was always a spring here, brought forth by the hydrology I have described; then the wall was built round it to stop wandering cattle trampling it into mud, and the stile and the steps provided for people fetching water from it to their beasts in nearby fields. This is a centripetal place; it draws one in and precludes the outward view. At its focus is the glint of the water that shows itself briefly before disappearing again into the earth.

There is another well a mile or so away, at the foot of the same scarp as An Poll i bhFolach and the well of Clochán an Airgid, and therefore strikingly similar to it in the formation of the cliffy slope above it. And here the mystery of water, its life-giving powers, is explicitly celebrated, for this is a holy well. In fact it is the well that inspired J. M. Synge's play *The Well of the Saints*. Its legend is the familiar one of the miraculous cure of blindness; Synge himself recorded it during his first visit to the islands, in 1898. A woman living in Sligo who had a blind son dreamed of the well and the cure in its waters, and took a boat and brought her son to Aran. She declined all guidance from the locals and went straight to the well, prayed, bathed her son's eyes – and saw his

face fill with joy as he exclaimed over the beauty of the
flowers around the well. This well is beside one of the
islands' most beautiful little medieval chapels, Teampall
an Cheathrair Álainn, the Church of the Beautiful Four.
These comely persons are by ancient sources identified
as Saints Fursey, Brendan of Birr, Conall and Berchan;
but I do not vouch for the historicity of their presence
here. It is fitting that legend names this well as Tobar an
Cheathrair Álainn, the Well of the Beautiful Four, for
beauty is the characteristic I want to retain from the
handful of places I have plucked out of the Aran Islands.
Now I'll go in search of a place with a different essence.

After I had made my map of the Aran Islands I looked
around me, and there to the east on the mainland were
the silver-grey uplands of the Burren. This is limestone
country too, of heavily glaciated karst, with fertile valleys hidden from each other by rounded or terraced hills
of bare, fissured, rock sheets. It is rich in prehistoric
remains; within say 150 square miles, there are 66 megalithic tombs and over four hundred circular enclosures
ranging from ruinous but still mighty triple-ramparted
cashels to slight walls that once enclosed the stockyards
of humble farmsteads. Many of these monuments are
almost drowned in thousands of acres of hazel scrub. To
force myself into every corner of this daunting territory
I decided to visit all the ancient sites marked on the old
six-inch-to-the-mile Ordnance Survey maps that were

my template, and in so doing I found many more antiquities. But it was a long, lonely struggle, often in foul weather. The Burren is often claimed to be a spiritual landscape, but if so it harbours an obstructive, secretive spirit among others, one who stretches brambles across paths, makes rock slippery with rain and confounds horizons with mist. Once, as I stood in the rain in a roofless church ruin, up to my knees in wet nettles, I was shown the severed head of a statue of a bishop, by an old man who seemed quite ready to demonstrate its use as a cursing-stone by turning it anticlockwise and so inflicting a stroke or a drowning on some enemy. Suddenly I felt a revulsion against the Burren, its obscurantist myths, its labyrinthine refusal to provide an intelligible view of itself, its slithery resistance to the grip of cartography. At other times its breezy, sunny hillsides, trembling with wildflowers and butterflies, were annexes to heavenly skies. And most frequently it drifted between these extremes, moody, ambiguous, as in the place I am going to describe.

A narrow road leads up out of one of the valleys of the central Burren onto a bleak plateau; I often had to push my bike up and across it. Scanning the plateau one sees an apparently endless recession of fields separated by breast-high drystone walls enclosing little but grey rock riven by fissures full of brambles and bracken. A solitary wind-inflected thorntree and a deserted single-storey farmhouse show on the horizon. The monotony of this area challenged me. There must be something hidden among these countless walls, I felt, something I can rescue from the nullity, the sterility, of mere location and mark on my map – for it is the attention we bring to it that makes a place out of a location. I used to leave my bike by the road and spend time straying to and fro among these anonymous fields. I never met anyone there. Then I came across a field that seemed worth recording, not for anything in it – the usual wind-shorn shaggy thistly stuff lurking in every crevice – but for the walls enclosing it. In many parts of the Burren it is easy to prise up large thin slabs out of the topmost layer of rock; the builders of megalithic tombs did it, and in Aran, which shares the geology of the Burren, the making of tombstones out of such slabs, and selling them to the south Connemara folk who do not live on limestone but on granite, was a thriving industry in the nineteenth century. Limestone is of course vulnerable to erosion; it is eaten away by the carbonic acid in rainwater, and any crack that water can penetrate will be enlarged over the centuries into a crevice many inches wide. Sometimes these crevices develop into gullies and basins of fantastic shapes. And this field had been fenced with slabs set on edge that exhibited – the word is right – a great variety of amoeboid piercings that would have pleased the surrealist sculptor Hans Arp. Look through these weird windows, and what is on one side is as lugubriously anonymous as what is on the other. I wanted to put this field on my map, but of course there was no way of indicating what was remarkable about it on the map sheet; nor did I want to make too much of it in a land of such marvels as the Burren. In the end I marked it with a dot and in tiny print the words 'a strange field'. Occasionally I hear from someone who has noticed this cartographic curiosity and gone in search of its objective correlative. Usually they have been unsure whether or not they found what I had found, or what it was they were supposed to see in it – but then there is nothing to be seen in it, just grey emptiness, nodding thistles, an occasional attendance of puzzled visitors on a mystique. I take from this instance another modality of places: strangeness.

From our little house perched on the skyline of Árainn we could look out across ten miles of sea to the ragged peninsulas and archipelagos of Connemara and its core of mountains. Nothing of the orderly levels of limestone here, instead an arrested flux and turbulence of upended and overthrown strata half quenched in a coastline of baffling intricacy. To map it seemed a reasonable conclusion to what already had become a totally unreasonable project of mapping all the land I could see from my home – as if I were so far lost that only a comprehensive universal map would find my place. At first my plan was merely to map that unmappably complex southern coastline, which I set out to walk from end to end, peninsula by peninsula, island after island, over a number of sessions of a few weeks each. This task, which seemed to impose itself like a ritual obligation of obscure significance, took so long that in the end we decided to move to the mainland and extend the map to include the mountains and the western, Atlantic, coast of Connemara as well. I was several years into this project when I came across the place I am going to select for description, out of Connemara's fecundity of place.

Gleann Eidhneach, the ivied glen, leads up into the centre of the cluster of mountains called the Twelve Pins. In the last Ice Age a glacier nested on a sunless north-facing slope of the mountain massif, and as it grew and inched downhill under its own weight it gouged out this wide flat-bottomed valley as a way for itself, before joining other glaciers coming down out of other mountain dens, and eventually finding its way to the sea. Ten or twelve thousand years ago it melted back, dumping thousands of tons of clay and boulders, a moraine that now lies like a rampart across the valley floor. A vigorous stream meandering down the valley has breached these drifts and flows through a little canyon twenty or thirty feet deep. Thousands of years of bog growth have carpeted the valley with heather and rounded the forms of the glacial moraine; bare rock shows only on the mountain slopes on either side. The place I would describe is perched on the smooth back of the moraine. I noticed it for the first time when walking up the valley in the company of an ornithologist; we were going to look for raven and peregrine falcon nests on the precipice at the head of the valley. We stopped to rest for a moment, and, idly looking before me across the valley, I saw six little vertebrae sticking up from the spine of the moraine, that aroused my curiosity. We splashed across a couple of hundred yards of wet bog and ran up onto the moraine, where we found a line of small boulders – a stone alignment in fact, a type of monument usually dated to the Bronze Age. The boulders were of the local quartzite; the largest, at the southern end of the row, was about waist high and contained a good deal of white quartz. I did not take much notice of the direction in which they were aligned – at first glance the row seemed to be pointing vaguely at the mountain wall on the south side of the valley. But when the trained archaeologists came along to verify my report of this find, one of them – Michael Gibbons – noticed that in fact it pointed at a V-shaped cleft in the high skyline, a high mountain pass leading over into the next valley. Further, he came back to the site on the shortest day of the year, the day of the winter solstice, when the sun's arc is at its lowest and the point at which it sets is at its southerly extreme – and found that, as observed from the stone alignment, the sun staged its farewell to the year exactly in that cleft. The following midwinter I went up the valley to pay my respects to this phenomenon. At two o'clock of the short winter afternoon the sun was blazing, but it was already in the grip of the mountains. Every minute detail of the

northern side of the valley, with its little potato plots straggling up the steeps from two isolated farmhouses, was
gold-washed, while the southern mountain wall was in
deep shade. The last of the sunbeams were so intense
that, looking along the alignment into the dazzlement,
it was hard to make out what was happening. As the sun
slipped slowly down into the cleft its radiance seemed to
erode the profiles of the slopes on either side. The flecks
of white quartz in the stones of the alignment almost
leaped from their beds in the flood of energy. Then the
sun was gone and the great mountain shadows stretched
out across the valley floor. The longest night was beginning; beyond that, the spring was already in waiting, and
all the annual phenomena of concern to the Bronze-Age
folk who had wrestled those boulders into position on
the crest of the moraine: the passage of migrating geese,
the warmth necessary for sowing corn, the salmons'
ascent of the stream. The calendar started from this day,
to which the alignment pointed as certainly as Christian
spires point to heaven.

But why was that alignment built exactly where it
was? For, if you think of it, as the setting sun moved
across the sky, the mountain shadow with the cleft in its
profile must have swept across quite an extent of the
valley floor, so that there would have been many other
points from which it would appear that the sun was setting into the cleft; an alignment in any of these places
would function just as well as the actual one as the focus

of a ritual or to mark the point from which the solstitial sunset was to be observed by some priest-astronomer of the valley community. But then the crest of the moraine is itself a proud place: it commands the valley floor and stands its ground in the face of the encircling mountains. If the spring wells I described from the Aran Islands are centripetal places, this Connemara site is centrifugal: vision is spun out from it, its mode of placehood is that of the outlook, the point of view. (Such observations belong to a field of study one could call distemics, the phenomenology of far-off things.)

But there is one defect in this grand spectacle of the solstitial sunset: the sun doesn't quite reach the bottom of the cleft in the horizon before disappearing behind the mountain to the west of it. If the stone alignment were a little further south, or the arc of the sun's passage across the sky were a little lower, the effect would be perfect, and even more dramatic. But consider this: The daily journeying of the sun from east to west is of course the effect of the earth's turning on its axis. A spinning top appears to bow in all directions, as every child notices; the orientation of its axis changes slowly, sweeping out a cone; the phenomenon is called precession, I remember from my mathematical days. So too for the earth, with complications – nutations, or noddings – due to its equatorial paunch, to the pull of the moon and the other planets; the upshot of these influences being that the angle of the earth's axis to the plane of its orbit round the sun changes cyclically by about two-and-a-half degrees, with a period of 41,000 years. This angle is presently decreasing, so that the midwinter sun seems to pass across the sky perhaps half a degree higher than it did say 3,500 years ago. So the Bronze Agers got their celestial architecture exactly right. In their day the midwinter sun, as seen from the stone alignment, disappeared precisely into the bottom of the cleft in the mountain skyline. (When I say 'precisely' and 'exactly', I am of course writing with the degree of precision one would expect of a row of boulders, rather than of a sextant.)

Making this mental correction to the spectacle of the midwinter sunset feels like adjusting the focus of an optical instrument, which is what the alignment, taken together with the cleft in the skyline, really is. From this perfectly placed place on the top of the moraine, a panorama of the mountain walls and the wide wild glen offers itself, and on the shortest day of midwinter another perspective opens up like the aperture in the dome of an observatory; one can see halfway to infinity and eternity, not only the dazzling millions of miles to the sun but the three or four thousand years back to the Bronze Age, and the forty-one-thousand-year wobble of the earth's tilted axis. The place is a foothold on a globe that is tumbling through space and time. The prehistoric links us back to the cosmic. Antiquity is the term I'll take to embrace both.

Do the virtually limitless depths of antiquity nullify our concerns with the present and the near future? Our barricades against global warming, whatever form they take, are hardly likely to be visible in the landscape in a few centuries' time. Also, we human beings have discovered a way of looking at time as if it were all spread out before us like the Bayeux tapestry, and the comprehensiveness of this vision consoles us for the narrowness of the segment of the panorama representing our own lifetimes. Nevertheless, like any other animal, each of us is the embodied origin of a particular perspective on time and space: what is near and soon concerns us with the urgency of a life we feel flowing away from us even as we live it. We are inescapably at the sharp end of this outlook, whether it extends into deep time or not. The tapestry model of time offers meagre protection; we can bundle it into a wad to blunt the point but we are still impaled upon the perspectives that constitute us.

Beauty, strangeness, antiquity – three fragile moments of place. The places I have described may stand for all the delicate facets of the earth that make it into the jewel of the known cosmos. None of the places I have conjured up for you out of the Aran Islands, the Burren and Connemara are in present danger. But you can imagine how a wind turbine up on that lonely plateau of the Burren would suck all the strangeness out of it and mince it up, and how the stone alignment and its literally spectacular relationship to topography and cosmology would fare if that magnificent valley were to be dammed to store up the 'Spirit of Ireland'. On the Aran Islands, with the decline of cattle farming and increase of building, a little unofficial quarry could obliterate a place like An Poll i bhFolach overnight; in fact the ravishingly beautiful well of Clochán an Airgid had a narrow escape from such a fate during our time on the island. And we are only at the beginning of society's reaction to the threat of global warming. What will be the pressures on us in a decade or two? Will irresolution be replaced by panic? For we have read dire predictions. Breach the recommended two-degree limit to global warming and we trigger a runaway process of positive feedback; at six degrees, say some, the vast quantities of methane presently safely tucked away on the ocean bed come boiling to the surface and ignite in a worldwide fireball. Improbable, but if anything like that happened, the earth would surely be screaming to be rid of us. Clearly we cannot be party to the extermination of all higher life, whatever it costs to avert it. And on the current modes of calculating that cost, the West of Ireland, whatever its stores of beauty, strangeness and antiquity, would be sacrificed. In which case what I have said about my three paradigms of place can be heard as an elegy for all lost places. I want to raise our awareness of what is at stake to a level approaching pain, a pre-emptive nostalgia for the places we love – and nothing sharpens the sensibilities so much as the threat of loss.

But the die is not yet cast. There is still time for a redirected human will, informed by a truly alternative set of values, to divert the course of events. So let my three descriptions be heard instead as a call to the defence of such places. And there is a special rightness in raising this call as from the West of Ireland, for a cult of place, or at least of placenames, is traceable in Irish culture from earliest times down to the present. The foundation myth of this cult is preserved in the medieval Irish text *Acallam na Senórach*, the Colloquy of the Elders. This compilation of stories concerning Fionn mac Cumhal and his warrior band the Fianna has as its framing device a wandering around Ireland undertaken by St Patrick in the company of Caílte, one of Fionn's band who has somehow long outlived his companions and is now submitting himself to the new order symbolized by the coming of the saint. At each of the forts and prominent landscape features they pass, Caílte pronounces its name and recites the events – usually bloody and uncanny – from which the name derives, and St Patrick commands one of his scribes to write them down for the edification of futurity. Thus the work enacts the passing-on of the Celtic Iron Age place-lore to the Christian dispensation – and although the text as it has come down to us is a product of monastic scriptoria it is filled with a sense of yearning for the great old days when the hunters revelled in the sights and sounds of the forest and the hills, and the doors of the otherworld lay open everywhere. *Dinnsheanchas*, as it is called, the lore of place, the exegesis of placenames, is a persistent feature of Irish literature, down to Brian Friel's *Translations*, in which a young British officer engaged in the first Ordnance Survey of Ireland in the 1830s, and an Irish peasant girl, having no common language, exchange as love-gifts recitations of the placenames each of them has grown up amongst.

However it must be admitted that this Irish fascination with placenames is too often purely nominal and does not extend to caring for the places themselves; nostalgia stands in for conservation and convenience trumps all. Here's an evocative list of placenames from a public notice I saw in a newspaper a few years ago. They are the names of townlands, the small land divisions that often equate to a single farmhouse and its land, or a hamlet, or a stretch of commonage:

Doughiska, Garraun North, Coolagh, Glennascaul, Frenchfort, Carnmore, Lisheenkyle, Barrettes Park, Caherbriskaun, Carraun Duff, Rathmorrissy, Pollnagroagh, Ballygarraun, Newford, Prospect, Baunmore, Gartnahoon, Furzypark, Farranablake, Boyhill, Toberconnolly, Loobroe, Moyode, Deerpark, Rathgorgin, Esker, Brusk, Carragh More, Greyford, Kiltullagh, Clogharevaun, Carrowroe, Ballynahown, Bookeen,

Carrowkeel, Clashagranny, Knocknaduala, Galboley, Carrowreagh, Killescragh, Caraun More, Cross, Cloonconaun, Rahally, Slievedotia, Brackloon, Rathglass, Owenavaddy, Treanbaun, Ballymabilla, Toormore, Gortnahoon, Cappataggle, Ballynaclogh, Slihaun Beg, Cloghagalla Oughter, Cloghagalla Eighter, Cooltymurraghy, Cloonameragaun, Coololla, Curragh, Barnacragh, Liscappul, Loughbown, Mackney, Garbally Demesne, Brackemagh, Moher, Dunlo, Pollboy, Tulrush, Ardcarn, Suckfield, Kilgarve, Beagh.

I wrote out this list as part of a letter to the *Irish Times* in 2004, suggesting that its readers might relish it. And I ended by saying:

> I don't know these little places, but I am sure they are as rich in variety and individuality as their names are, even in these anglicised forms. But this is the list of townlands to be torn through by the proposed N6 dual carriageway from Ballinasloe to Galway.
>
> Read the list again, and weep.

But that was in boom-time Ireland, the Old Woman of the Four Green-Field Sites. The paper did not publish my letter, and nobody wept. In fact from visitors to Connemara I hear nothing but praise of the new road, which reduces the driving time down from Dublin to three hours or so; and indeed if I had to do that journey often I'd feel the same. Ours is the age of the shortcut, trading space for time; technology is shortcuts, ever abridging the gap between intent and fulfilment. And technology, having hurried us into the present crux of global warming, now offers to deliver us from it, in return for the ground from beneath our feet. But before we sacrifice the 'hole in hiding' (taking that tender spot in the Aran Islands to stand for all the places liable to be brushed aside by the renewable energy industries) there is much we can and should give up, if necessary by going the long way round, by abjuring some of the shortcuts of technology. I might suggest that war, the ultimate (but often delusive) technological shortcut in its impatient abandonment of the serpentine ways of diplomacy, is a luxury of which we could be sparing. (In discussion of the rights and wrongs of current and recent wars I don't remember seeing their carbon footprints mentioned, although they must be gigantic.) But I don't feel called upon to design the carbon-frugal, place-conserving economy we need; that's for the experts, including right-minded technologists. However, per-haps I can say something about the re-evaluation of place that might motivate such a project.

First, the role of placenames. Reverting to that list of places knocked about by the new dual carriageway: they are given in their anglicized forms, but in most cases one can recognize the original Irish-language versions

underlying them. These are both musical and meaning-
ful. Dabhach Uisce, water hole; Lisín Coille, little fort
of the wood; Baile an Gharráin, the village of the
thicket; Gort na hUamhna, field of the cave; Eiscir —
an *eiscir* is a ridge of glacial deposits marking the course
of a river that flowed under the ice of the last glaciation;
Sliabh Dóite, burnt mountain; Ceapach an tSeagal, the
rye plot; Clocha Gealla, bright stones; Lios Capaill,
ringfort of the horse . . . all pregnant with history
and topography. To idealize a linguistic situation that in
reality is often ravaged and corrupted, a placename
summarizes the place's attributes and origins, asserts its
excellencies and rights to respect. Therefore the handing down and rehearsal of its placename is a place's
first defence against neglect or exploitation, against its
being regarded as a mere shortcut to some other more
profitable place. Among the historical roots of Ireland's
carelessness of place is the retreat of its language and
the accompanying anglicization of its placenames, which
have been defaced, rendered dumb and sometimes reduced
to the ridiculous. To undo a little of this damage has
been for me, an Englishman, a work of reparation.

One reason I have found the placenames of Connemara and the Aran Islands so fascinating is that they are
for the most part in the Irish that is still current, and
that my access to the language is limited, so that they
appear to me as so many secrets to be unveiled, riddles
to be solved, clues to a mystery, passwords to a cult.

And with the word 'cult', a tinge of the religious comes in again. What might a cult of place entail? One could take guidance from the ancient cult of holy wells – with which I have become very familiar, my map of Connemara being constellated with the dozens of holy wells I have been shown, many of them known only to a few old folk of the immediate vicinity. The cult involves visiting, thoughtfulness, ritual handling of pebbles, water, flowers – as well as features we can do without: superstition, penitential barefootedness, repetitive mumblings. A secular version might call forth an awareness of the place's constitution, the causal net that brought it into existence, from cosmic origins to the casual touch of local microhistory. On such occasions the basic act of attention that creates a place out of a location would be renewed, enhanced by whatever systems of understanding we can muster, from the mathematical to the mythological, by the passion of poetry, or by simple enjoyment of the play of light on it. Here is a gateway to a land without shortcuts, where each place is bathed in the sunlight of our contemplation and all its particularities brought forth, like those mountainside potato plots gilded by midwinter sunset in the valley of the stone alignment.

I bring this suggestion forward with some hesitation, being uncomfortably aware that to propose the cult of holy wells as a model for our times might appear quaint, hopelessly antiquated, terminally rustic. Have I sojourned too long in Connemara? But, reading through the descriptions of the three places I have given you, I note that in each case I have spontaneously drawn on imagery of pilgrimage and shrine. Realizing that the mindful seeking-out of place has been the half-subconscious drive of my practice in all these years of mapping and topographical writing, I can hardly disown this terminology now, unbeliever though I be. And since for centuries the material world was seen as a quarry of metaphors to describe the glories of a spiritual world, that gorgeous structure of the imagination should in return provide the liturgy and ceremonial we need for a praiseful approach to the places that glorify the here below.

Placenames, whether they exist in the mind of the Irish *seanchaí*, the custodian of traditional lore, or in the memory banks of a database, are only the anchor points of a discourse of place. To create a language for the secular celebration of the earth, with the height and power of the religious tradition but purged of supernaturalism, can be seen as the task of ecoliterature, tracked and made conscious of itself by ecocriticism. But can literature submit to being welded to any particular aim or study in the way these awkwardly compounded terms suggest? A better word might be 'geophany', with its echo of theophany, the manifestation of a deity, or the celebration of such an appearance. If I have to call on the terminology of religion it is because that is the language evolved to address the highest; and the highest is what lies under our feet and bears us up. Geophany, then, the showing forth of the earth through all the geophanic arts and sciences, should be our means towards a reformation of values. The secretive beauty of Aran's spring wells, the strangeness of the ragged little fields of the Burren, the deep antiquity of the stone alignment in Connemara, stand here for the countless precious things for which we will be mourning, if in ten or twenty years' time we find we have sacrificed them to the technology of shortcuts, in a misdirected effort to save the world.

Notes

Hunter-gatherers, written 2015. All true to life.

On Ilkley Moor, written 2015. Autobiographical.

How I Learned to Love the Police, written 2015. Told exactly as it happened.

As the Cicada Sings It, written 2012. True to my childhood observations, and to J.-H. Fabre, *Souvenirs Entomologiques*, 1879–1909.

Contrescarpe, written in the Centre Culturel Irlandais, Paris, 2011. Quotes from *L'Astragale*, Albertine Sarrazin, 1965, and *Contrescarpe*, Julien Sarrazin, 1977.

Byzantium, written 2015, amended 2018.

The Centre of Gravity, published in *Archipelago*, 2015; autobiographical apart from the 'note' forming its centre of gravity.

The Gods of the Neale, published in *Archipelago*, 2013. My adventure occurred in 1979, is truthfully recounted in the first section, and successively departs from truth in the second and third sections.

Where are the Nows of Yesteryear? Inspired by argumentation overheard in the Moral Sciences Department,

Cambridge, in 2011–2012, and published in *Connemara and Elsewhere*, ed. Jane Conroy, 2014. The famous query, 'Where are the Snows of Yesteryear?' is due to Dante Gabriel Rossetti, after Villon.

The Tower of Silence, written 2013 and published in *Connemara and Elsewhere*, 2014. The first part is factually correct, and all the items of human interaction in the second part were observed by the author as recounted.

Parallax, written 2012 (?). The description of my father's mannerism is true to life.

Shadows and Eclipses, written 2016. The description of seeing the egg in the museum and its subsequent disappearance is true to facts, but there is no indication of the origin of the lecture that crashes into this episode.

Orient Express, written 2012. Autobiographical up to the moment of decision, after which – diagraphical might be the word.

Two Cries, Two Cliffs, written 2016 and strictly factual.

Backwards and Digressive, autobiographical, written 2015.

A Land Without Shortcuts, written 2010–2011 as the Parnell Lecture; delivered in Magdalene College, Cambridge, 2011; published in the *Dublin Review*, Spring 2012.